# THE MANI

Text, Illustrations
and Cover Photographs
by
Bob Barrow

Published By:-
Antonis Thomeas Services
Stoupa, Messinia, Greece
Tel: 0030 (0)721 77689  Fax: 0030 (0)721 77571
E-Mail: anthom@otenet.gr

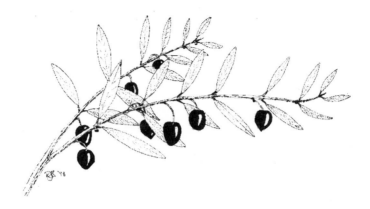

For My Daughters

## *SHIRLEY AND LUCY.*

"My thoughts are many miles away -
They lie with you when you're asleep
And kiss you when you start your day."
(Paul Simon - 'Kathy's Song')

For My Daughters

SHIRLEY AND LUCY.

"My thoughts are many miles away -
They lie with you when you're asleep
And kiss you when you start your day".
(Paul Simon - 'Kathy's Song.')

# TABLE OF CONTENTS

Maps

Antonis Thomeas Services

# MAPS

If you have bought a map of the area, do NOT take it for granted that "What you see is what you get". Many show roads that aren't there, that are little more than tracks or might be there one day - but not yet! Some appear to show "three lane highways" over the Taygetos Mountains but these are pure fiction! The maps in this book are my own and I am no cartographer. For this reason, the scales are "approximate" and there are no contours or colour grades to show elevation. They should, however, get you where you want to go.

Having said that, many of the roads are being upgraded and better signposts are appearing all the time. You may well find that I have described a track which has since been improved and surfaced or that my attempts to describe a route have been made much easier by improved sign-posting.

# THE MAIN PENNINSULA

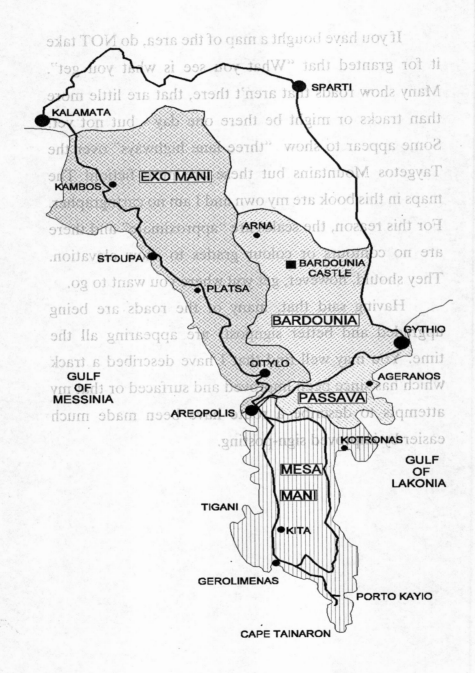

- SPARTI
- KALAMATA
- EXO MANI
- KAMBOS
- ARNA
- STOUPA
- BARDOUNIA CASTLE
- PLATSA
- BARDOUNIA
- GYTHIO
- OITYLO
- GULF OF MESSINIA
- AGERANOS
- PASSAVA
- AREOPOLIS
- KOTRONAS
- GULF OF LAKONIA
- MESA MANI
- TIGANI
- KITA
- GEROLIMENAS
- PORTO KAYIO
- CAPE TAINARON

# EXO MANI

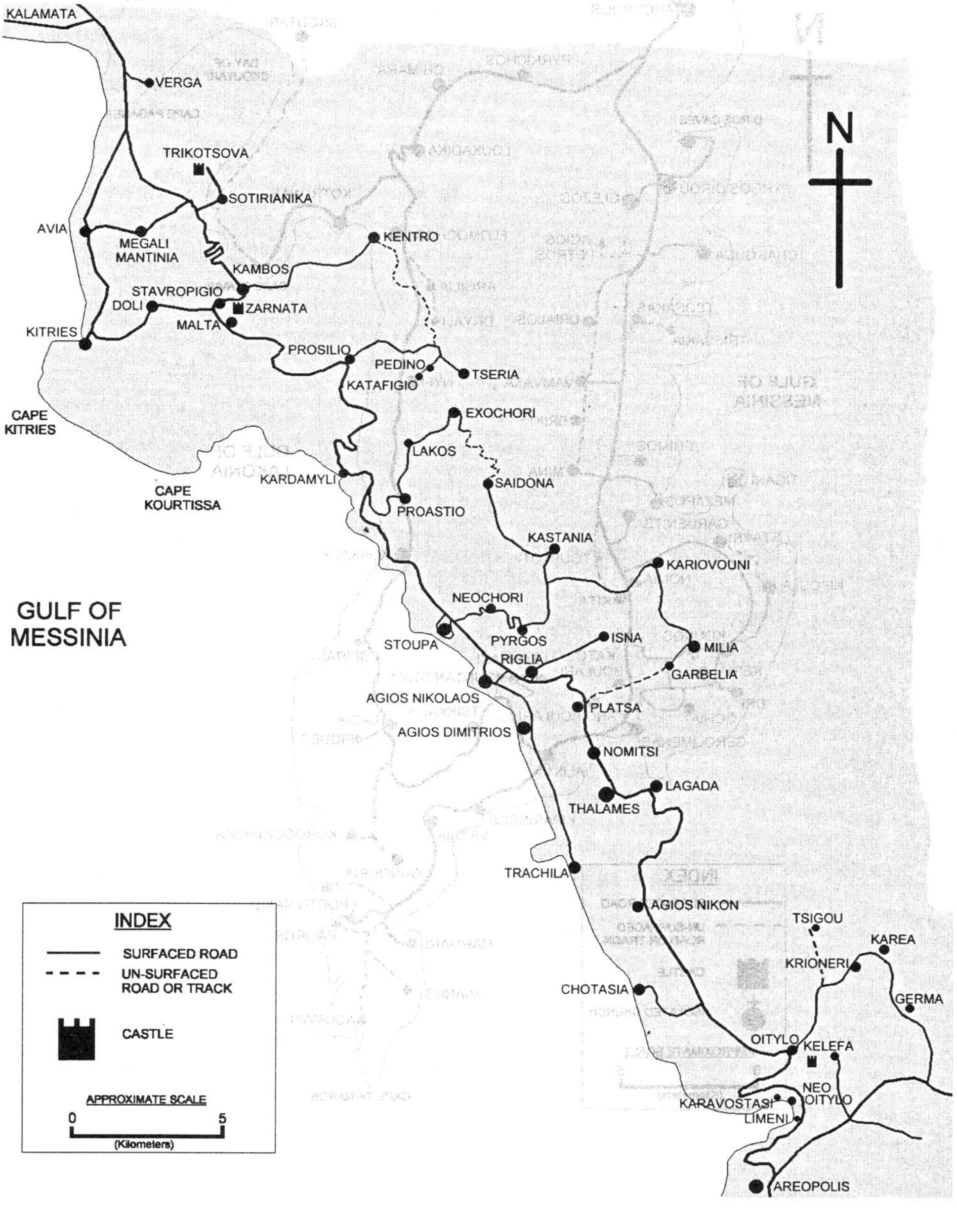
KALAMATA
VERGA
TRIKOTSOVA
SOTIRIANIKA
AVIA
MEGALI
MANTINIA
KENTRO
KAMBOS
STAVROPIGIO
DOLI
ZARNATA
MALTA
KITRIES
PROSILIO
PEDINO
TSERIA
KATAFIGIO
CAPE
KITRIES
EXOCHORI
LAKOS
SAIDONA
KARDAMYLI
CAPE
KOURTISSA
PROASTIO
KASTANIA
KARIOVOUNI
GULF OF
MESSINIA
NEOCHORI
STOUPA
PYRGOS
ISNA
MILIA
RIGLIA
GARBELIA
AGIOS NIKOLAOS
PLATSA
AGIOS DIMITRIOS
NOMITSI
LAGADA
THALAMES
TRACHILA
AGIOS NIKON
TSIGOU
KAREA
KRIONERI
CHOTASIA
GERMA
OITYLO
KELEFA
NEO
OITYLO
KARAVOSTASI
LIMENI
AREOPOLIS
N
INDEX
SURFACED ROAD
UN-SURFACED
ROAD OR TRACK
CASTLE
APPROXIMATE SCALE
0
5
(Kilometers)

# MESA MANI

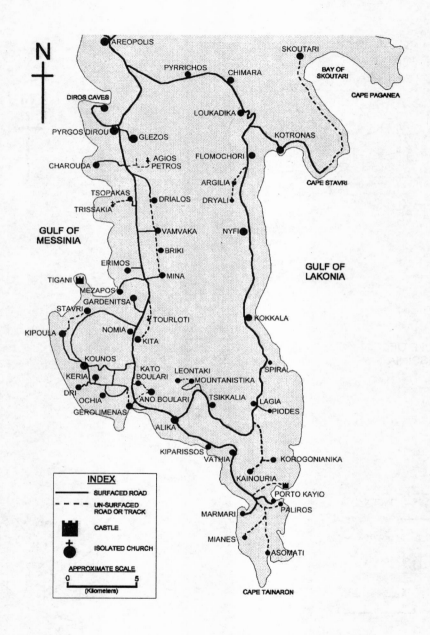

AREOPOLIS

SKOUTARI

PYRRICHOS
CHIMARA

BAY OF
SKOUTARI

CAPE PAGANEA

DIROS CAVES

LOUKADIKA

PYRGOS DIROU
GLEZOS

KOTRONAS

AGIOS
PETROS

FLOMOCHORI

CHAROUDA

CAPE STAVRI

ARGILIA

TSOPAKAS
DRIALOS
DRYALI

TRISSAKIA

GULF OF
MESSINIA

VAMVAKA
NYFI

BRIKI

ERIMOS

GULF OF
LAKONIA

TIGANI

MINA

MEZAPOS
GARDENITSA

STAVRI
TOURLOTI

KIPOULA

NOMIA

KOKKALA

KITA

KOUNOS

KERIA

KATO
BOULARI

LEONTAKI
MOUNTANISTIKA

SPIRA

DRI

OCHIA
ANO BOULARI
TSIKKALIA
LAGIA

GEROLIMENAS

PIODES

ALIKA

KIPARISSOS
VATHIA
KOROGONIANIKA

KAINOURIA

PORTO KAYIO

MARMARI
PALIROS

MIANES

ASOMATI

CAPE TAINARON

## INDEX

——— SURFACED ROAD

- - - UN-SURFACED
ROAD OR TRACK

🏰 CASTLE

⛪ ISOLATED CHURCH

### APPROXIMATE SCALE

0       5

(Kilometers)

# PASSAVA AREA

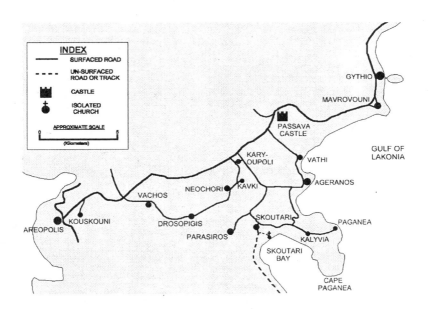

# BARDOUNIA AREA

PASSAVA AREA

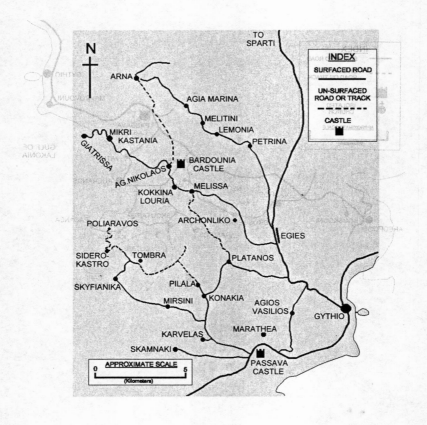

# GENERAL INFORMATION

## 'EXO' AND 'MESA' MANI

The Mani Peninsula is divided into 2 main regions - Exo Mani and Mesa Mani - which literally mean 'outer' and 'inner'. The dividing line is generally accepted as running from Oitylo to Gythio with Exo Mani to the north and Mesa Mani to the South but, for the sake of simplicity and journey planning, I have used the road from Areopolis to Gythio as the boundary.

To the east of the Taygetos Mountains, I have further subdivided the area into "Passava" and "Bardounia". You may also come across references to "Sunny" and "Shady" Mani which represent East and West of the Taygetos mountains respectively.

## PAUSANIAS

There are many references to Pausanias (Pronounced Pavsaneeas in Greece) in this book. He was a Greek who travelled extensively throughout Greece and Asia Minor in the 2nd Century AD, during the Roman Period. Most of the classical temples and sanctuaries were still intact and in use and he kept a record of all that he saw in his travels. His books have proved invaluable for identifying archaeological sites and as a record of the religion and culture of Classical Greece. All the references used are from Book lll: Lakonia or Book lV: Messinia and taken from "Pausanias - Guide To Greece", Volume 2 - Southern Greece, as translated by Peter Levi and published by Penguin Classics. It is an extremely interesting publication and the notes which Peter Levi has added are very informative. No "Grecophile" should be without it!

## COLONEL W.M. LEAKE

W.M. Leake like Pausanias, travelled extensively through Asia Minor and Greece and through the Morea and Mani in 1805. He virtually ignored Byzantine culture but made notes and observations on the possible locations of Classical Sites, using Pausanias as his main reference. He also recorded anecdotes and observations about the Maniats and their customs and seemed quite surprised and relieved to have survived his travels among them - "Thus terminates my journey in the land of Evil Counsel (Mesa Mani) without accident or any loss except that of a double-barrelled pistol which was stolen out of my holster on the 12th." He was an Army Colonel and obsessed with timing, and his notes are meticulous in this detail - "April 14th. At 6.30 I leave Alika: at 7.35 pass between the villages called Ano Borali and Kato Borali. At 8 pass again between Nomia and Gita the polypyrgous. At 8.35 cross the torrent of Mezapo ....."

His book, "Travels in the Morea" was published in 1830 in 3 Volumes and although it is out of print, you might find it in a library.

## THE EARL OF CARNARVON

The Earl of Carnarvon jouneyed into the Mani in 1839 and like Col. Leake, kept a journal in which he recorded all that he saw and heard. His observations provide an insight into the life of the Mani after the War of Independence but before acceptance of centralised government and the erosion of culture and tradition. The notes, compared to the pre-war notes of Leake, highlight the fact that very little had changed although the Turkish threat had been removed.

## THEODOROS KOLOKOTRONIS

I also frequently quote Kolokotronis who is known affectionately as "The Old Man of the Morea" - the Morea being the name used originally by the Franks for the Peloponnese. He is splendidly portrayed on the current 5,000 Drachma notes and was the leading General in the Peloponnese during the War of Independence. Prior to the war, he was very much involved in Exo Mani, especially in the mountains behind Stoupa, and a seasoned campaigner against the Turks. He was proud to be a 'Klepht' - now a word meaning little more than thief or bandit, but which in his day signified a man who continually resisted the Turkish occupation from mountain refuges. To quote from his book, "The name of Klepht was a boast. 'I am a Klepht', some would say vauntingly. The prayer of a father for his son was that he might become a Klepht. The Klephtship afterwards lost its authority. In my father's time it was a sacred thing for a Greek to undertake."

He was a remarkable man who endured great hardship throughout his life with only one purpose in mind - the liberation of Greece. He served under the British in the Ionian Islands and here learned 'modern' warfare as opposed to the Guerilla warfare of the Klephts. He was proud that he always wore the 'fustanella' - the pleated skirt which is the national costume of Greek soldiers and men. His service was rewarded by the British who promoted him to the rank of Major and the lessons he learned served him well in the battles to come against the Turks.

After the war, he was accused of treason and sentenced to death for allegedly plotting against the new Regency. This was commuted to twenty years imprisonment to which he is said to have responded, "I shall cheat the Regency for I shall not live the twenty years." He was pardoned by King Otto as soon as he assumed the throne and enjoyed the trust and friendship of the King for the last ten years of his life.

# TERMINOLOGY

## TOWER HOUSES, TOWER DWELLINGS, WAR TOWERS

I have used these terms to distinguish the different types of tower:-

A "Tower House" is a dwelling reinforced by a defensive tower which was usually only occupied in emergencies - with the possible exception of the lower floors. The tower was normally built onto the end of the house but there are cases where the tower was added to the side of the house and occasionally with a house on either side of the tower. They usually had internal access from the house to the tower.

A "Tower Dwelling" is a much wider tower with larger windows which was built to be permanently lived in but retained the defensive character of a tower. It was not necessarily linked to a house. These are mainly 'newer' towers built after 1833.

A "War Tower" was built purely for 'military purposes' and is usually free-standing among family or clan houses within a 'stronghold'. Apart from sentries, it would not be lived in except in time of conflict.
I also refer to houses as being 'defensively built'. They were essentially dwelling houses without towers but with small, high windows and with doors which were small and difficult to enter. They often had defensive features such as described below.

## ZEMATISTRA
These were stone projection on walls, usually above a doorway, and protected holes which pointed downwards from which gunfire or boiling water or oil could be directed at anyone attacking the doorway.

## KLOUVIA or VIGLES.
These were round turrets or sentry posts projecting from the corners of towers and houses. They usually incorporated 'DOUFEKOTRYPES' - loop-holes from which to fire a gun and 'Zematistra' (see above).

## PETRAMACHOS.
These were rectangular projections from walls with Doufekotrypes and Zematistra. They were often constructed above doorways to reinforce their defence and were sometimes built onto the lower halves of windows. They were also used as lavatories when occupants were unable to leave the building during an attack or siege.

## TOWER HOUSES, TOWER DWELLINGS, WAR TOWERS

I have used these terms to distinguish the different types of tower:-

A "Tower House" is a dwelling reinforced by a defensive tower which was usually only occupied in emergencies – with the possible exception of the lower floors. The tower was normally built onto the end of the house but there are cases

Left - Agii with open window

Right - The window sealed for war

where the tower was added to the side of the house and occasionally with a house on either side of the tower. They usually had internal access from the house to the tower.

A "Tower Dwelling" is a much wider tower with larger windows which was built to be permanently lived in but retained the defensive character of a tower. It was not necessarily linked to a house. These are mainly 'newer' towers built after 1833.

A "War Tower" was built purely for 'military purposes' and is usually free-standing among family or clan houses within a 'stronghold'. Apart from sentries, it would not be lived in except in time of conflict.

I also refer to houses as being 'defensively built'. They were essentially dwelling houses without towers but with small, high windows and with doors which were small and difficult to enter. They often had defensive features such as described below.

### ZEMATISTRA

These were stone projection on walls, usually above a doorway, and protected holes which pointed downwards from which gunfire or boiling water or oil could be directed at anyone attacking the doorway.

## GOUVA

The partially underground, vaulted base of a tower with access only from within. This was used for storage and sometimes as a prison and access was by trap door and ladder.

## CHORA

This was the term used to describe a group of villages or hamlets in one local area and is still sometimes used today.

## MEGALITHIC BUILDINGS

These literally mean made of "large stones" and dating them is an ongoing project. Some of the megalithic houses in the Mani area might be as old as the Neolithic period (4000-2000 BC) but the method of building continued much later. For example, there are Megalithic churches which are thought to belong to the Mid-Byzantine and Late Byzantine period (10th-13th century). The term Megalithic therefore describes a method of construction rather than a period of history.

## THRESHING FLOORS

These were circular, paved areas, still commonly seen on the outskirts of villages, where wheat or barley were threshed.

## TIKLES

The 'slate' roofing tiles of older houses and churches.

## KALDERIMIA

(Pronounced kaldereemia). Old, cobbled or paved donkey or mule tracks that connected the villages and towns before the 'modern' roads were built. They were 'stepped' in steep areas and sometimes crossed small stone bridges. Many still exist although stretches have been destroyed by the construction of the roads.

## "STONE PILES"

Many people are curious about the stones they see stacked one upon the other and usually on top of a dry stone wall, a prominent rock or even a post. They are frequently whitewashed as well. These are markers to show shepherds and goatherds that they may NOT graze their flocks on this piece of land.

## ROAD-SIDE SHRINES

The common 'myth' is that these are erected by family members in memory of someone who died in an accident at that spot. They are in fact erected by people who survived an accident here and are dedicated to the particular Saint associated with their name and who probably intervened to save them.

# CHURCHES

Sadly, many of the churches you come across are now kept locked because thieves have plundered them of their frescos and marble decorations to sell to 'art lovers' of the world. Local enquiries can often reveal a key-holder.

## CUPOLA

The circular or polygonal, domed 'turret' on many churches. Strictly speaking, the walls of the turret are called the 'drum' and the roof is the cupola but I refer to the whole construction as the Cupola. This building style developed in the 7th Century and required a structure strong enough to support a drum and cupola above a square, open area. This was usually achieved by building on two wall sections on either side of the main apse and on two columns or by supporting the structure on four columns.

## NAOS

The central area or 'nave' of the church.

## ICONS

Icons are literally 'images' which were originally painted wooden panels depicting various Saints or Holy Images.

## ICONOSTASIS & TEMPLON

This is the wooden screen which partitions the Naos from the Sanctuary. Iconostasis literally means "Icon Station" and it is an ornately carved and decorated structure with Icons displayed on it. When constructed with masonry or marble, as in earlier churches, this screen it is called a Templon.

## GYNAIKONITIS

An area in a church reserved for women. This was usually at the rear of the church and in some took the form of a gallery built above the floor of the church.

## OSSUARIES

Most grave-yards have a small building in the grounds. These contain boxes in which the bones of the deceased are stored, having been disinterred from graves which are then used again - a practical solution to the problem of digging in rock and a custom which may derive from taking the bones of ancestors to a new site should the occupants of a village have to move elsewhere by choice or circumstances. (Please do not give in to morbid curiosity and respect the privacy of these places).

It is worth having a look around the outside of a church (or old house) as they often have interesting relief carvings and 'etchings' on the walls. A popular theme seems to be sailing ships. You will occasionally see pieces of carved, classical marble built into the walls as a result of what some archaeologists call "quarrying" - re-using materials from disused buildings.

In antiquity, fountains and springs had a religious significance and Pausanias on his travels usually noted the springs which had names and were often linked to a sanctuary or a temple. When Christianity replaced the 'pagan' religions, the same sites were frequently adopted to ensure that they replaced the old religion and did not exist alongside it and even The Parthenon in Athens was converted to a church. For this reason, you frequently find churches near wells and springs and at Nomitsi, a church was even built on top of the existing fountain. This adaption of religious sites may also explain why some churches are often found in remote or isolated areas, away from villages or houses, as with those found on mountain peaks.

Greek Orthodox churches are usually built with the altar facing East. Where you encounter a church with a different orientation, it could signify that the church has been built on an old ruin - often a former temple.

# A BRIEF HISTORY OF THE MANI PENINSULA

The Mani is the southern-most peninsula of the Peloponnese and is rich in History and Tradition. On the western side, the peninsula extends from Kalamata on the northern shore of the Bay of Messinia to Cape Tainaron, the mythical entrance to the underworld and the most southerly tip of mainland Greece. On the eastern side, the rugged coastline extends north from Cape Tainaron to Gythio and the eastern slopes of the mountains above the plain of Sparta. The entire area is dominated by the vast grey mass of the Taygetos Mountains (pronounced Ta-eegitos) which form the spine of the peninsula and which have dominated the lives of the people of this ancient region and its history.

The Taygetos are a formidable natural barrier which have provided a refuge from, and a centre of resistance to, the various forces that have invaded and conquered Greece in the last two thousand years. The caves at Pirgos Dirou provide evidence of habitation in the area since the Stone Age and Homer's Iliad lists the towns of the region that supplied men and ships for the Trojan War during the Mycenaean (Bronze Age) period. The area was probably a refuge during the Dorian invasion of the Peloponnese and in Classical times most of the area was under the control of Sparta - a heritage of which most modern Maniats are very proud.

In the Hellenistic period, Sparta's power and domination declined, Lakonia was repeatedly invaded and Philip V of Macedon penetrated deep into the Mani in 218 BC. Twenty two years later he was defeated by the Romans who crushed Sparta the following year and made Gythio the main city of a league of free cities to counter-balance Spartan power and influence. This Union of Free Lakonian Cities was officially recognised by the Emperor Augustus and Pausanias in his travels in the second century AD described these flourishing cities and other sites in his travels through the area.

In 330 AD , the Emperor Constantine made Byzantium his seat of Government and renamed the city Constantinople. His successor, Theodosius, kept the Empire formally intact but the two main cities, Rome and Constantinople, were polarizing on religious grounds. The diverging interpretations of the life and nature of Christ led to the formation of the Roman Catholic Church in the west and the Orthodox Church in the east. When Rome fell to Alaric and the Goths in 410, the eastern half of the Empire, including the Greek Peninsula, survived as The Byzantine Empire with Constantinople as its capital and the center of the Orthodox Church.

There is debate as to when the Mani was converted to Christianity but it is probable that isolated pockets on the coastal areas were converted in the 6th

Century AD, prior to the less accessible mountain areas, and there is reference to the Mani being a Diocese in the 9th Century AD although complete conversion probably did not occur for another 100 years or so.

The Slavic invasions of the Peloponnese resulted in more people seeking refuge in the Mani and although these invaders did penetrate parts of the Mani Peninsula, they do not seem to have reached the southern area in any great force.

In 1204 the Fourth Crusade attacked, sacked and looted Constantinople. Originally destined for Palestine, or Outremer as it was known, to rescue the Holy Places of Christendom from the infidels, this barbaric Crusade diverted to this rich and civilized Christian capital to loot and plunder its great wealth. Although the city was recovered in 1261 and a new Byzantine Dynasty, the Palaiologoi established as emperors, parts of the empire remained occupied by western powers until the conquest of the whole of Greece by the Ottoman Empire.

Geoffrey de Villehardouin had already landed in Syria when the news reached him of the diversion of the Crusade to Constantinople. He set out for the city at once, worried that he would miss out on the spoils, but was driven west by winter storms and finally made a landfall at Methoni on the peninsula west of the Mani. Early the next year, he met with Guillaume de Champlitte at Nafplio and together they set out to conquer the southern half of the land they called the Morea as most of the North Peloponnese had already been subdued by Boniface of Montferrat.

This quest was continued after his death forty years later by his sons, Geoffrey II and Guillaume (William). William completed the conquest in 1248 when he captured Monemvasia after a two year siege but he was still plagued by a fierce Slavic tribe, the Meligs, who were established on the heights of the Taygetos. To control them, he built the castles of Mystras, Great Maina at Tigani and Beaufort at Lefktra (Stoupa).

At the battle of Pelagonia in 1259, William was completely defeated and taken prisoner. Within two years, the victor of this battle, Michael VIII Palaiologos, had recaptured Constantinople and William was forced to cede his great castles as a ransom for his release. The southern Peloponnese was once more part of the Byzantine Empire, with the exceptions of Methoni, Koroni and Nafplio which had been sold to the Venetians, and remained in their hands until the Turkish occupation of Mistras in 1460.

There had been many refugees in the Mani over the years but the most influential were the Byzantine families who came to the area after the collapse of Mistras. An elite known as the 'Nyklians' rose to supremacy and various families developed fortified enclaves which either controlled the entire village or . adjoined a similar enclave of another Nyklian family within the village. The barren landscape was unable to support the population and for the next four hundred years the clans fought bloody feuds for control of the meager resources and to dominate their locality. Just how crowded this area was is illustrated by the remarks of the Earl of Carnarvon who recorded in 1839, "In spite of the perpetual warfare which has devastated the Maina, I have not seen so many villages from Athens to Marathonisi (Gythio) as from Marathonisi to Tsimova (Areopolis). Indeed I think I have seen more between Tsimova and Kita than between Tsimova and Athens."

The intensity and ferocity of these feuds resulted in the unique architecture 'The Tower Houses' which dominate so many of the villages in the Deep or 'Mesa' Mani. A description of the lifestyle that led to the development of the towers was recorded by A.G. Guillet in 1676: "As each one is a veiled enemy of everyone else and usually the closest neighbour is the worst enemy, each night one member of the family stands guard on the roof of the dwelling. Otherwise the neighbour comes over on purpose, lifts a tile and makes an opening to shoot those who are sleeping. Cases are known where someone found the opportunity to dig a hole under his enemy's house  they filled it with gunpowder like an explosive charge and blew up the entire family." He also recorded the pirate activities of the Maniats as being a "festival for the Maniats" and that they used "small boats, easy to sail and drawing little water".

Only Nyklian families could raise tower houses or ordinary houses with marble roofs or with "kamara" - vaulted roofs - and from these towers, the clans, who were often based in the same village, carried on their blood feuds and vendettas. There were further 'building restrictions' and the permitted height of an ordinary house used the 'kalami' as a measure. This was the height of a man with his arm raised holding a length of cane. (Kalami literally means 'cane' or 'reed'). If they were higher, the owner was forced to pull down the top part until the house complied with the restrictions. In this way, the elite families controlled the defensive capabilities of their inferior neighbours. This inferior social group was called the Achamnoteroi  and relied on the Nyklian families (also known as the "Megaloyenitai" or great families) for protection.

The feuds were conducted according to established rules and the main objective was to kill as many of the opposing family's men as possible and wipe them out or force them to surrender. To do this in a closely confined village, one family would try to build their tower higher than their opponent's and using muskets, cannon and rocks - try  to smash the marble roofs of their houses and effectively neutralise them. Simultaneously, the constant barrage of bullets and small cannon were used to kill as many of the male members, 'the Guns', of the opposing family as possible. So the towers grew higher and can still be seen in many of the old villages in both Mesa and Exo Mani. Where the feud was with a family from further afield, ambushing members of the family and their supporters was the approved method and occasionally, if one side felt strong enough to succeed, they would launch an all-out attack on the enemy's tower.

The Maniats themselves acquired a reputation for ferocity and courage that was second to none and every man was always armed with as many weapons as he could manage. In 1600, a French traveller described them as follows: "These mountain dwellers are so laden with weapons that they look like hedgehogs. A huge sword is not enough for them, they carry a gun on their shoulder and in their hands they hold an axe, a club and a short spear." In addition, they often carried two or three primed pistols in their waist sashes.

The same feudal hierarchy existed in the Outer or 'Exo' Mani but with less rivalry. Here the villagers would accept a family as their Kapetanios and this heredity would go unchallenged. There are tower houses in Exo Mani but villages do not bristle with towers as they do further south at places such as Kita or Vathia. In Exo Mani, the strongholds of the Kapetanios tended to be organised in defensive positions that resemble small villages themselves, such as the Troupakis 'complex' at Kardamyli or the former complex at Kitries.

Obviously the towers and complexes proved to be good defences against the Turks as well as neighbouring clans and J. B. S. Morrit observed, "The country admits not of the conveyance of artillery and their towers, ill calculated as they may seem for the improved warfare of more polished nations, offered a powerful means of resistance against the efforts of the Turks and had more than once materially delayed their progress."

The feuding was encouraged and prolonged by the Turks as it weakened cohesive efforts to resist their occupation. They invested power in one clan leader, granting him local autonomy and the title of 'Bey' and it thus became the Bey's problem to control the Mani. This ploy, however, did not enable them to subdue the Mani as those they appointed continued to maintain Maniat interests and the dream of Greek freedom, while seeming to support Turkish interests at the same time.

The first two Beys, Zanetos Koutifaris of Zarnata (1776-1779) and Michael Troupakis of Kardamyli (1779-1782) were both lured on board ships for a 'conference' and then beheaded by the Turks for their failure to control the Mani. The third, Zanetos Grigorakis of Gythio and Mavrovouni (1782-1798) not only negotiated with the French for support against the Turks but also helped the escape of a notorious pirate, Lambros Katsonis, who had been attacking Turkish ships from his fortified base at Porto Kayio. He was deposed by the Turks and Koumoundouros of Zarnata (1798-1803) was made Bey.

To cause disruption among the Maniats and within the Grigorakis family, he was removed from office four years later and Zanetbey's nephew, Antonios

Grigorakis of Ageranos (1803-1808) was made Bey. Koumoundouros would not accept this and, helped by Theodoros Kolokotronis, resisted a Turkish force which attacked his tower at Kambos. Koumoundouros was taken prisoner and sent to Constantinople where he died but Kolokotronis, although wounded, managed to escape.

Antonbey was also deposed because the Turks thought he was helping the guerilla efforts of his uncle, the former Zanetbey, and Pantelis Zervakos (1808-1810) was made Bey. He was pro-Turkish so the Maniats refused to accept him and drove him out of Mani. He was killed by the Turks in Constantinople for his failure and replaced by Theodoros Grigorakis of Mavrovouni (1810-1815). This appointment of yet another member of this family caused great discontent in western Mani and so power was then transferred to Petros Mavromichalis of Limeni (1815-1821). He made contact with the Philiki Etairia - the secret society that was plotting a revolution against the Turks throughout Greece - despite the fact that his sons were held hostage in Istanbul. Petrobey then negotiated with the Kapetani of the leading Mani families and in 1821 he secured a 'treva' or truce among the families and united them in the common cause of revolution.

On 17th March 1821, he led his forces out of Tsimova, which they renamed Areopolis, City of "Ares" - the God of War, and marched up the Mani to Kardamyli where he joined forces with Kolokotronis, Mourtzinos and the Messinian Maniats. They attacked the Turks at Kalamata on 23rd March, securing the first victory in the war which finally liberated Greece after hundreds of years of foreign occupation.

The Maniat interpretation of Independence did not encompass the whole of Greece but rather Independence for themselves and their way of life. They did not take kindly to the idea of taxation and control by a central government of Greece - any more than they had accepted the same from the Ottomans - and consequently the family feuds and opposition to government interference continued for some time.

The first President of Greece, Ioannis Kapodistrias, angered the Mavromichalis clan, especially when he denied the Maniat Kapetani the right to collect customs duties at their ports, and imposed a government tax on them. In 1830, a revolt was fermenting in Limeni and rumours were circulating of a Maniat attack on Nafplio, the capital of Greece at that time. Petrobey was a virtual hostage at Nafplio and when he tried to leave, was captured and imprisoned. This action subdued the revolt and a delegation was sent to Mani to negotiate peace with the clan and persuade the eastern Maniats, who were preparing for a war with the clan, to remain where they were and not to attack. However, the Mavromichalis clan were still not satisfied, especially as Petrobey was still being held prisoner, and so Kapodistrias was assassinated at Nafplio in

September 1831 by Georgios and Konstantinos Mavromichalis, the son and brother of Petros, who were subsequently executed for this crime.

Greece remained highly unstable but was recognised as an independent kingdom in 1832, under the protection of France, Russia and Great Britain. They gave Otto, the son of Louis I of Bavaria, the throne of Greece but, as he was only seventeen years old, regents were appointed until he came of age in 1835.

In 1833, the very soul of Maniat culture came under attack when it was decreed that the Mani towers would have to be pulled down. The situation was made worse by rumours that the Greek Orthodox Church was under threat from Bavarian Catholicism, and by the arrest of Kolokotronis on charges of treason. The first attempt to enforce this decree in 1834 resulted in a detachment of Bavarian troops being surrounded, forced to surrender, stripped naked and ransomed for a derisory price. A second attempt by a larger Bavarian force resulted in heavy losses and a forced withdrawal. A third attempt with 6,000 regular troops again failed to enforce the order and a negotiated settlement resulted in the order being rescinded and the towers were left intact. Many towers were built after this time but they tended to be wider and designed to live in as well as retaining their defensive character.

In 1839, the Earl of Carnarvon recorded the Maniat dissatisfaction with the new state. "Many even, in their disgust at the new civilization which had promised so much and done so little, which had destroyed political and feudal power, and which had given no compensation in the form of material prosperity for what it had taken away, were tempted to regret the days of Turkish rule, when a rude autonomy prevailed." In other words, many felt they had more freedom, more self determination, under the Turks than under their own Government.

The last great Maniat family feud was finally brought to an end as late as 1870, when a detachment of regular troops, supported by artillery, were sent to Kita and forced two families to stop fighting each other. From here on, the history of the Mani reflects that of modern Greece but the individual character of the peninsula, and its inhabitants, remains unchanged.

# MANI TRADITION AND CULTURE

In classical times, the Mani was not very different from the rest of Greece. The real contrast with the rest of the country developed after the fall of the Roman Empire and the subsequent invasions which hastened the collapse of the Byzantine Empire and, ultimately, domination of the rest of Greece by the Ottoman Empire.

Survival in the crowded Mani depended on power and that in turn depended on ownership of land and water. Out of this constant struggle evolved a unique culture with its own traditions. It was undeniably violent but so was life elsewhere on the Peloponnese, especially for those who resisted Turkish domination, as Kolokotronis illustrates in his autobiography when he gives examples of the consequences of being captured alive by the Turks during his time as a Klepht. "Old Gianni Kolokotrones was killed at Androusa (Messinia) - his hands and feet were cut off , and he was then hung." The same fate awaited "the old father of Panagioras" who was eighty years old. He was captured alive after a stalwart defence of his tower at Kastanitsa - "The hands and feet, however, of the aged warrior were amputated, and he himself was afterwards hung."

A drastic preventative measure was also used among friends, - "When any of us was seriously wounded in a battle and could not be carried away, we all kissed him and then cut off his head. It was thought a great dishonour to have the Turks bear away one's head." It is against this backdrop that the Mani acquired its reputation but it maintained a degree of autonomy not experienced elsewhere in Greece - and survived.

# FEUDS AND TOWERS - PRIESTS AND PIRATES

The struggle for power in the Mani was rooted in the need to obtain and control areas of valuable land and then to defend them against others with equal ambitions and the method of defence that evolved was the Tower. This was explained by Col. Leake when he wrote, "Each person of power and every head of a family of any influence has a pyrgo (tower), which is used almost solely as a tower of defence: the ordinary habitation stands at the foot of it. ...in general these buildings are uninhabited except in times of alarm. To overturn the pyrgo of the enemy and to slaughter as many of his relations as possible, are the objects of every war. The tower has loopholes in the different stories and battlements on top, and he that can get a rusty swivel (small canon) to plant upon them is not easily subdued. Most of the ordinary dwellings are built with loopholes in the walls; nor are the villages in which there is no inhabitant of sufficient opulence to build a pyrgo, the more peaceable on that account, but quarrel either among themselves or with their neighbours, and endeavour to overturn one another's houses just like their betters."

The evolution of an elite, feudal society in tightly confined boundaries with local autonomy required its own system of justice. The lack of any organised district government meant that a system of personal rendering of justice prevailed and this was known as "Aftothikia" whereby matters were resolved within the family. Aftothiko literally means - "to take the law into one's own hands" and from early beginnings in the 15th Century, it evolved into a highly structured process. Before enactment , a family would first consult its oldest members and, if sanctioned, would then give warning of the decision to the offending family. From then on, all and any actions were considered just. This did not usually mean an all-out attack on the enemy but would more often take the form of ambush and murder and this was considered perfectly honourable. This method of warfare could result in a feud continuing for a great number of years with "tit-for-tat" ambush and murder until the virtual extinction of one family.

This in turn led to the creation of "rules" to enable the normal cycle of life to continue, although that may sound like a contradiction in terms. The harvest was essential to survival so a "treva" or truce could be called to enable the crops to be gathered and sometimes "safe conduct" would be granted to a rival provided he was accompanied by a third party who was trusted by both sides to act as escort. The feud could end in a truce, sometimes by the intercession of a third party, or by the families themselves with a mutual pardon. This was done to prevent the virtual extinction of both families and the mutual pardon removed the obligation for vengeance.

In general, women and priests were not direct targets and could come and go unharmed. Thus the women's role also included the supplying of food, ammunition and powder to the family tower when under siege and running short of supplies. The Earl of Carnarvon recorded, "The Maniats never attacked a woman. In the fiercest wars, no shot from tower or ambuscade (ambush) seems to have been directed against her. Even when she served as a screen for her husband, the assailed party is said never to have returned fire upon her." This was not entirely true for there were instances where the pregnant wife of a murdered man would be deliberately killed to prevent possible future vengeance from a son.

Aftothikia was given moral support by the church in Mani - if only by keeping silent. It was the only form of justice available and the priests were usually natives of Mani who had been raised within the tradition. Most had received only local training and had not attended any major religious centres, so their acceptance of Mani life was no different from other inhabitants. In reality, what could the church have done to prevent the feuds? The Earl of Carnarvon asked the same question and wrote "My Maniat friend observed that they (priests) would have been in danger had they interfered, but that they pursued a prudent course in saying that they had nothing to do with points of honour." Besides, the Maniats themselves were usually very devout and adhered strictly to their Christian beliefs as Col. Leake observed when he wrote, "No people are more rigorous in the observances of the Greek Church than the Maniats. A Kakavuliote (Maniat from Mesa Mani), who would make a merit of hiding himself behind the wall of a ruined chapel, for the purpose of avenging the loss of a relative upon some member of the offending family, would think it a crime to pass the same ruin, be it ever so small a relict of the original building, without crossing himself seven, or at least three, times."

The Earl of Carnarvon also remarked on this contrast between strict religious observance and casual disregard for killing. "I was eating some fowl in one of their rude dwellings on a Friday. 'I would not do that for all that the world could give me,' said a young Mainote chief, who had been much with me, and whose hands were red with a hundred murders.

'But,' observed my muleteer, with the freedom so common in these countries, 'you would think nothing of killing a man.'

'Oh no,' replied my Mainote friend, 'but eating meat on a Friday is a crime."

Not only did the church condone Aftothikia, but by acknowledging it as the only available system, on occasion resorted to the use of it themselves. Col. Leake recorded an incident which occurred two months before he went to the Mani, when the son of a priest had accidentally killed a boy who was related to another priest. "The latter papas declared war against the former, which is done in Mani in a formal manner, by crying out in the streets. The first papas went to his church to say mass with pistols in his girdle; such being a common custom in Mani; but as usual in such cases, he laid them behind the altar, on assuming the robe in which the priest performs divine service. The other papas entered the church with some of his party, and the instant the office was concluded, walked up to his enemy, who was still in his robes, and fired a pistol at him, which flashed in the pan (failed to fire properly): the latter, then running behind the altar, seized his arms, shot his enemy and one of his adherents, and drove all the rest from the church. The affair was then settled by the interposition of the Bey himself, in whose village it had happened."

Another example of the church tolerating and even condoning activities which would seem to be the reverse of doctrine elsewhere, was concerning piracy. The Maniats were famed and feared as pirates and the coastline of the peninsula was a place for shipping to avoid whenever possible. The peninsula had been subjected to raids throughout history and piracy was considered a legitimate response to this and also provided goods which would not otherwise be available and for which there was never the money to trade. Not only were the pirate boats blessed by the priests to encourage success but priests frequently accompanied the boats on their forays and raids.

Such a violent existence, which also included fighting off invaders and raiders, took a heavy toll of manpower and the greatest asset to any family or clan was the amount of men who could fight on its behalf. The birth of a son, often called a 'gun', was a major event and the birth of a daughter was by contrast, a virtual disaster. This paramount need for men resulted in large families as Leake said when he stayed at the tower of Katzanos in Skoutari, "Katzano has twenty five persons in his family, of whom nine are his children; he married at the age of nineteen, his wife was fourteen; they have had fifteen children." If a wife failed to provide sons, the husband could marry again, without a divorce from the first wife, and if the second wife bore sons, they were considered legitimate.

The Earl of Carnarvon attended a wedding in Kita where he was told that the first wife had not had any children, so the groom was taking a second wife. "On my asking some further questions, it appeared that his first marriage had indeed given him three daughters; but my informant repeated his statement that there were no children - so completely are girls counted as nothing in this country. One of my muleteers clinched the argument by the additional question of - how could a man wish to have anything to do with a woman who brought him no sons?" This attitude conveniently overlooked the role that some women had played in warfare - not least of all at Pyrgos Dirou in 1826 when women saved the day against a Turkish invading force of 1,500 men - only 13 years prior to Carnarvon's visit and only a few kilometres away!

Leake also reported that many women were good shots and one offered to put a musket ball through his hat at 150 yards range but he declined. "I had too much regard for my only hat to trust her, for she has had two wounds in battle, and affects to consider her husband as no braver than he should be." He also told the story of a woman defending her tower against a Turkish force while covering the escape of a servant and her two children through a back door. In fact, the courage and fighting ability of women in the Mani was indisputable and the Earl of Carnarvon acknowledged this when he wrote about meeting Petrobey Mavromichalis's mother, "a most interesting person, who had with her own hand fought against the Turks, and on more than one occasion had defeated them."

There was another side of Maniat life which appears to be almost a contradiction of the fierce reputation acquired by the Maniats as pirates, mercenaries and brigands - the tradition of hospitality. "Nor less sacred was the virtue of hospitality." wrote the Earl of Carnarvon, "Poor themselves, and barely deriving a subsistence from their rugged soil, they would accept any privation or make any sacrifice for the humblest stranger who might claim their assistance." Leake also encountered unreserved hospitality wherever he went and none more so than when he met an old priest at Kiparissos, "whose only costume is a jacket with a pair of wide trowsers of course blanketing of Maniat manufacture, receives me with an air of cheerfulness and hospitality;" After describing his obvious poverty, Leake goes on to say, "He points, however, without hesitation, to the only fowl he possesses, as he desired us to "take off its head", imitating the action of a Pasha ordering an execution."

Another facet of Mani culture was superstition and The Earl of Carnarvon records many examples of this. It may seem logical that men who held life so cheap might well be haunted by the ghosts of their victims but this is not the case - as Carnarvon takes pains to point out. They were not haunted by their deeds and held in disdain any ghost of a victim of theirs - "Why should we care for the ghost of an enemy." are the words of a Maniat soldier as recorded by the Earl.

Superstition in the Mani mainly took the form of demons which haunted certain places and the activities of witches. For instance, the Earl wrote of an incident where he picked up a fresh egg at the road side and offered it to a soldier in his escort who took it willingly and then returned it very quickly. The reason given for this was that it may have been  bewitched by an old hag and whoever ate it might be forced to marry her!

The superstition which I find the most surprising was the belief in Vampires which, like their Transylvanian cousins, sucked the blood from the living and eventually caused their death. Carnarvon was shown a house where the owner, a shoemaker, had returned from the grave every night except Saturday night and, as well as making a few shoes, had made his wife pregnant! When accused of infidelity to her husband's memory, she told them the cause. "At this horrifying disclosure," wrote the Earl, "the villagers sallied forth to attack the Vampire in his tomb, undertaking the enterprise on a Saturday morning, on which day alone the Vampire's devil-imparted strength forsakes him, and the grave has power to hold his body. They found him working in his grave, making shoes. "How did you know I was  a Vampire?" exclaimed the still living tenant of the tomb. A villager, in answer, pointed to a youth whose cheek a month before had been bright with health, but on which the ghastly paleness of disease and coming death had fixed its mark. The Vampire immediately spat at him. The moisture from those accursed lips burnt the man's capote (jacket) as though it had been fire, but it could not hurt the man himself, because it was blessed Saturday." The Earl continues the story with the Vampire threatening the entire village with vengeance so the villagers tore him to pieces, cut out his heart and divided it into portions which were distributed and eaten by the villagers - this being the sure and proven method of disposing of his kind.

An earlier superstition, which was recorded in a letter from the Bishop of Monemvasia to the then Byzantine Emperor, prior to his visit to the Peloponnese in 1415, was the practice of severing the finger of a murdered man and soaking this in a glass of wine to ward off evil spirits. Superstition still exists but, as far as I know, in less drastic form - rather like "walking under a ladder" or Friday 13th. I once gave a lift in my car to three Papas or Priests and when I told a Greek friend, he was horrified. Giving a lift to one Priest was inviting bad luck and he hated to think what could happen to me after having three in my car! I don't know why Priests are considered unlucky but Patrick Leigh Fermor in his book about the Mani talks of the possible bad luck when a priest boarded the same boat that he was on and the effect this had on other passengers and crew. "Gorgons and Centaurs" - Chapter 13 of the book - is a fascinating study in which he attributes superstition to a continuation of the pagan beliefs of Ancient Greece.

The violent lifestyle of the Mani meant that death was a constant companion and in virtually every household or family there would be a widow wearing black. In this harsh landscape, death served to perpetuate a tradition as old as Greece herself - the funeral dirge or Miroloyia - which is still practised today. I have no experience of these dirges but D. Eliopoulou Rogan explains them very clearly in her book "Mani: History and Monuments". (Out of print) - as does Patrick Leigh Fermor in "Mani".

There are technical differences in the Miroloyia of Exo and Mesa Mani. The dirges of Exo Mani are lines of fifteen syllables and are adapted from a well structured formula which can be altered to suit the age, social position and circumstances of the death. This format is similar to funeral dirges from other parts of Greece

In Mesa Mani, the dirges have eight syllables per line but the main difference is in the composition which is personal to the deceased. Like an ancient tragedy, the women express their grief in spontaneous poetry, often accompanied by tearing their hair and scratching their arms and faces. The astonishing thing is the ability of poorly schooled and even illiterate women to create "epic poetry" which in days not long passed, was often used to urge their men-folk to seek the vengeance of Aftothikia if the deceased had been killed by another family. The poem would also relate the strengths and weaknesses of the dead man, his achievements and failures and frequently attributed the latter to broader political and social issues of the day.

The singing of dirges and lamentations was also done by the women while at work in their homes in the evenings - usually while grinding corn with small hand-mills. Col. Leake recorded, "The chief instrument of household furniture is the handmill, in which the kalambokki (corn) is ground. This is the employment of the women at night, who generally accompany the work with a song of lamentation of some deceased relation who has been killed, perhaps by a hostile house." The Earl of Carnarvon also encountered these chants while staying at Kita. "Late in the evening I heard the women in the Demark's house grind the corn. As they turn the machine they accompany the motion with a wild and plaintive, and somewhat monotonous song, generally composed by themselves in memory of some family event. The words now sung were in honour of a brother who was killed fighting bravely at Tripolizza (Tripoli). Sometimes, of an evening, the town of Kita resounds with the strains of such wild chaunts."

So the Mani was a barren, violent, place where the struggle to survive forged a culture that held life cheap but was deeply religious; where hospitality was inviolate but piracy honourable; where women counted for little but, illiterate as they were, could spontaneously create an "epic poem". It is an awareness of these contrasts or paradoxes that makes this region so fascinating for me and I hope this chapter will help you to understand and appreciate what you see on your travels - not least of all why a landscape studded with war towers also contains so many beautiful Byzantine and post-Byzantine churches with carved marble and frescos that show great artistry and devotion.

HANDMILL & STORAGE JARS

# THE TOWNS AND VILLAGES OF EXO MANI

## KALAMATA TO KAMBOS

There are three ways to get from Kalamata to the Kambos area, crossing the "frontier" as it were, in Verga which is generally considered to be the entrance to the Mani.

## VERGA

As you leave Kalamata, heading south for Mani, you pass through Verga and, on your left by a bridge, you will see a large white marble statue of a Maniat Warrior. Running up towards the mountain slopes from here is an old stone wall with many Polemotrypes (firing loops) built into it and then you reach a derelict, round tower with polemotrypes and larger openings for cannons. The wall used to run several hundred metres further, straight up the mountain and there was also a square tower on the other side of the road towards the sea but these have disappeared - probably due to 'quarrying'. The wall runs along the top of a dry riverbed and this combination presented a formidable obstacle to the Turkish attackers.

This type of 'linear defence' is called a Verga and hence the name of the area. It was built in a very short time under a system known as "maziki" - together - whereby everybody helped to raise the defence in the same way that many towers were built at short notice with mutual collaboration within a family or clan.

In June 1826, the War of Independence was going badly for the Greeks and Ibrahim Pasha, the Egyptian general who was supporting the Turks with his army, was poised to attack the Mani. He had swept through the Peloponnese after the fall of Missolonghi (where Lord Byron had died of a fever) and seemed to be invincible. News of his approach caused the wall to be hastily built and manned by the Maniats to thwart his intentions. He was defeated at Verga in a fierce battle which lasted for four days and was forced to withdraw to Kalamata when Kolokotronis approached over the Taygetos Mountains with a force of 2,000 men. The Pasha had simultaneously landed another force behind the Maniats at Pyrgos Dirou to attack them from the rear but this force was defeated by Maniat women who attacked it with stones, knives and sickles. (see Mesa Mani - Pyrgos Dirou). Proof yet again, if proof were needed, that even a well devised and executed military attack against the Mani can still fail against the determination and courage of the Maniats of both sexes.

There is a strange footnote to this incident. En route to Verga, Ibrahim Pasha stopped at Messini where he had a disturbing dream. A local lady, Mrs. Sykous, had a reputation as an interpreter of dreams and, when consulted, predicted impending disaster for Ibrahim. After his defeat he returned to Messini and ordered Mrs Sykous to be hanged in the square!

## THE DIRECT ROUTE SOUTH

Just beyond Verga, the road splits at a Y junction and you take the left fork to stay on the main route south towards Kambos. The road starts climbing up into the mountains in a series of long zig-zags and you have a dramatic view across the Bay of Messinia to the shore of the peninsula opposite and of Kalamata and Messini at the north end of the bay. After about 6 kilometres, you reach a small hamlet with a few houses and Kafeneon on either side of a straight stretch of road. If you look to the north, you will see Trikotsova Castle perched high on a hill above this small hamlet. Just past the bend at the end of the straight stretch of road is a turnoff to the left, signposted Sotirianiaka and this road takes you through two small villages and then a tarmac road runs right up to the castle itself. The views from here are magnificent and the castle is interesting to walk round.

## TRIKOTSOVA CASTLE

I can find very little on the history of this castle other than it belonged to a powerful local family - Kapetanakis - one of the Kapetanios or regional governors. Leake lists Yiorgos Kapitanakis as the Kapetanios governing all of Zarnata and based at Stavropigio, so the family seem to be controlling a large area in 1805. The castle was completed in 1795 although some additional work was done prior to the War of Independence. For example, above the main gateway you can see where the battlements have been raised higher.

The castle sits impressively at the summit of a steep, rocky hill commanding the route from Kalamata. The main feature is a 3 storey tower surmounted by battlements and with four Klouvia on the corners. Access to upper floors of this tower would have been a very difficult task for an attacker - as you will discover if you decide to enter it. One side of the tower forms part of the east wall of the castle, close to and protecting the main gate. On the other side of this gate, at the corner of the castle where the east wall joined the south wall, is a smaller round tower, again with battlements which have been raised. Next to this and forming part of the south wall is a small church. There is another, smaller gate in the wall at the end of the church and again you can see where the battlements have been raised, making the wall a more formidable prospect to an attacker.

Two sides of the castle (the north and west walls) are formed by two large oblong, two storey buildings which originally would have housed the garrison and would traditionally have had a large communal reception hall. There is another small door in the north wall. These buildings had battlements on the inner walls as well as the outer walls so that the large courtyard could be defended should an attacker manage to break through any of the gates. It is against such an eventuality that the first floor of both buildings could only be reached from the courtyard by stone steps which could be more easily defended. The ground floor, like virtually every house or dwelling in Mani, was for the stabling of animals. There are small, round Klouvia where the corners of these buildings formed the outer corners of the castle.   There are no buildings within the courtyard but the mouths of two large underground cisterns are raised above ground level.

The main road continues past the Sotirianika turnoff towards Kambos, approximately 11 kilometres from here and, shortly after passing a small white church on your right, the road drops down into Koskagos Gorge and winds its way up the opposite side. The Gorge is spectacular and spanned by a fairly modern concrete bridge, directly beneath which is an old, single arched, Venetian bridge - just wide enough to take donkeys and mules in single file. It is not easy to see from the road but a track leads down from the road on the north side of the gorge to the stoney, usually dry, river bed if you want to have a closer look.

The road meanders south from the gorge until you reach Kambos. There is a petrol/service station on the outskirts of the town and another on the main street through the town. (There are no other petrol stations until Kardamyli and no "unleaded" petrol until Stoupa).

## ALTERNATIVE ROUTES TO KAMBOS
## ROUTE 1 - VIA MEGALI MANTINIA

There are two other routes into Mani and they are off-shoots of the coastal road which runs from the right fork of the Y junction which is just past Verga. The coast road is lined with houses, apartments and tavernas and just past Avia, is a turnoff to your left, signposted Megali Mantinia.

Avia takes its name from ancient Avia which Pausanias says "used to be called Ire and was one of the seven cities Homer makes Agamemnon promise to Achilles." He explains that the name was changed to Avia in honour of Herakles' (Hercules') nurse who founded a sanctuary here to her former charge. He also says there was a sanctuary of Asklepios here but these have never been identified or excavated. The road takes you up through the olive groves to the village of Megali Mantinia with a large, derelict church by the roadside. The road continues and then joins the main route north of the turning for Sotirianika.

## ROUTE 2 - VIA KITRIES AND DOLI

Kitries lies further down the coastal road, beyond Avia. This used to be a very important anchorage and walled complex and was the base for five of the Beys of the Mani. It was completely destroyed in an earthquake and no trace remains of this once extensive fortification. Leake visited Kitries before the War of Independence and said, "The pyrgo of the Bey and adjoining buildings are large and agreeably situated on a height above the sea. Besides the Bey's pyrgo and its dependencies, the only buildings at Kitries are five or six magazines (shops) near the sea. In one of these I found a singular personage, a Turk keeping a shop in a country of Greeks."

Lord Carnarvon visited Kitries in 1839 and recorded, "We passed the ruined aqueducts and fountains which marked the scene of much former splendour." His host, Petrobey Mavromichaelis's brother remarked that the government "disputed him even the possession of his own house, battered as it was by Ibrahim Pasha's guns; and his means were too low to allow him to restore the ruins."

Nowadays Kitries is a very peaceful and attractive fishing village with a small harbour and a couple of Tavernas and, although nothing remains of the fortifications, it is well worth visiting.

To reach Doli, you must backtrack for a kilometer or so along the coastal road to a turnoff on your right which directs you to Kalianeika, Doli, Kardamyli and Diros. This road is quite narrow and rough in places but it is "driveable". As usual, you have wonderful views as you wind up the hills and through the small village of Kalianeika. The strange, low stone buildings you will see here are covered cisterns where rain water was collected. Climbing higher, you reach a tiny, Byzantine church on your right with a Kalderimi running alongside it. Judging by the icons inside, this is dedicated to Agios Nikolaos and, although it has been recently restored, some of the frescos remain. A little along the road, you will see a barrel-vaulted church on your left with a corrugated roof. It has been concrete rendered inside and out so keep going towards Doli which is approximately 5 kilometers from the coast.

Doli is really two villages - Ano and Kato Doli - and the first one you reach is Kato Doli. The approach is through a very picturesque area with many Cypress trees but sadly most of them are infected and many are dead or dying. You will see many ailing trees in the region and they are infected with a disease which I'm told originated in California.

To enter Kato Doli, you turn left at the T-junction  The church here is dated 1800 and has some fine decorations externally but a new concrete bell-tower. It is hard to park in the village and I found nothing else of particular interest. The road goes through the village and down towards the shore but turns into a track after about one kilometer. It is signposted Kitries and Kalamata but I have never been down it.

If you turn right at the junction, after a short distance there is a road to your left signposted to Ano Doli. I have a copy of a print dated 1830 which shows Doli (both parts) as having two churches with massive pointed spires. These have disappeared and the church at Ano Doli has been 'restored'. It is dated 1805 on the smaller bell tower and there are frescos above the doors. The rest has been plastered over.

This alternative route emerges onto the main route at the southern edge of Stavropigio and you turn left, through the village and down the hill to Kambos.

NOTE FOR WALKERS. Kambos is probably as far as you would get comfortably in one day from Kalamata, but there is very little in the way of accommodation here. I would recommend you take the bus from Kalamata to Stavropigio (just beyond Kambos) and take the Kalderimi to Kardamyli where you will find ample accommodation. The walk is wonderful, the views rewarding and it's much more fun than tramping along the highway. The Kalderimi starts on the outskirts of Stavropigio, to the right of the road, shortly after the turnoff to Doli and the route is marked with daubs of yellow and blue paint. Walking time is about 3 hours.

**KAMBOS**

The village of Kambos is dominated by two features which are both visible from a long way off - the large church and the castle of Zarnata on the hill above the village. The village itself is on either side of the main road with Kafeneons and a couple of small shops lining the road. There is a sharp right hand bend at the far end, and just past this you will see a small Byzantine Church on your right. It is dedicated to the Saints Theodoros and they are depicted on a fresco above one of the doors. The other door has some very attractive carved decorations and a few frescos have survived inside the church.

Pausanias describes a city he calls Gerenia and Homer called Enope - one of the cities that sent ships to Troy and which was offered to Achilles by Agamemnon during their dispute at the siege of Troy.  It is believed, but not proved, that Gerenia was Zarnata or Kambos or both. (In fact there is much academic discussion between archaeologists as to the location of Gerenia - some place it at Kitries and name Kambos as Alagonia).

Pausanias reported that Nestor was brought up in this city (Gerenia) or he took refuge here and that there was a memorial to Asklepios' son, Machaon, together with a sanctuary for healing. This place was called the Rose and had a statue in bronze of Machaon. He also recorded that Mt. Kalathion was in the territory of Gerenia with a sanctuary to Klaia (a nymph) beside a sacred cave "narrow at the entrance but with interesting things inside." It has never been found and it is very frustrating that he did not record what the "interesting things" were!

On the left hand side, half way down the main street is the turn-off for Kendro which takes you past the large, domed church in the centre of Kambos. It is an impressive sight from a distance but disappointing when up close.

**THE ROAD TO KENDRO**

Behind Kambos, the road climbs passed a village, Vorio, (Oraves on some maps) on your left on top of a small hill. It is a quiet little village and the church was locked so I cannot report on that. As you climb higher towards Kendro there are fantastic views of Kambos, Zarnata and beyond. You finally cross the barrier of hills into a valley shaped like a basin with villages perched on the slopes.

**KENDRO**

Kendro seems to be a collective name for these villages which lie quite close together. It is marked on some maps as Gaitses or Chora Gaitses. It may be the City which Pausanias called Alagonia - one of the Free Lakonian Cities - where he recorded sanctuaries of Artemis and Dionysos. Inscriptions have been found here to Apollo and Caracalla, a Roman Emperor. The location has never been proved by archaeological finds but nowhere else fits Pausanias's directions quite so well. The name Artemis is still very popular here and a Greek friend suggested this may well be because of the sanctuary of the goddess.

Kendro was attacked by the Turks in the 17th Century but there are no obvious defences other than the difficult approach to the valley and the slopes on which the villages are sited. The first village is on the edge of the Koskargos Gorge and the scenery is awesome. Park by the church in the small square and walk towards the gorge and follow the path which takes you east along the top of the gorge. From here you have a panoramic view of the mountains and the gorge with the Bay of Messinia in the distance. The other villages have old houses and narrow winding roads and the whole area is so peaceful it seems cut off from the real world. Don't be tempted to take the road towards Tseria over the mountains. It starts well but deteriorates and has a high puncture risk so return to the main road at Kambos.

## KOUMOUNDOUROS' TOWER

Travelling south from Kambos the road climbs uphill at the base of Zarnata Castle and on your right you will see a ruined tower dwelling. It was originally a windmill (the round end) but was turned into a fortified building, constructed so that the entrance was flanked by part of the tower and defensive fire from upper windows could protect it. There is a tale that the tower was connected to Zarnata Castle by a tunnel but I don't think so. It would have been a huge engineering undertaking without any real strategic necessity, vulnerable to earthquakes and I can find no historical reference to it.

In the early 1800's, Theodoros Kolokotronis was wounded while fighting here for the Fourth Bey, 'Koumoundouraki'. The Turks had deposed him as Bey in favour of Antonbey Grigorakis and had sent an army to subdue him. Kolokotronis recorded in his biography, "The chieftains and other Maniats fought with us and I was wounded but we took possession of a tower and during the night we reached the fort." (Zarnata). Koumoundouros was forced to submit and taken as a prisoner to Constantinople where he died but Kolokotronis escaped capture.

In 1870 it was another family member, Alexandros Koumoundouros who, while Prime Minister, used troops to end the last great Maniat feud at Kita. Just below the tower - to the right as you look at it from the road - are the remains of a Mycenaean "tholos" or "beehive" tomb. The conical roof has collapsed but the entrance, surmounted by a massive stone lintel, is still intact and the interior walls show how the tomb was constructed with the courses of stones diminishing towards the centre to form the "beehive".

## STAVROPIGIO

Continuing up the hill from the tower, just over a kilometer from Kambos, you reach the village of Stavropigio which has narrow winding alleyways and many old houses which you need to explore on foot. The village is also the best access to Zarnata Castle. On a right hand bend in the main road, you will see a small cafe on your left with a sideroad running straight up into the village. There is a T-junction a little further along this side street and here you turn left up a narrow street with old houses on both sides until you reach a small square with a church immediately in front of you. Pass this on the right side and continue a little further. Where the road starts to bend to the right, there is a track running up the hill past some new houses and this takes you to the summit of the castle. It is only a ten minute walk from here as opposed to scaling the heights from Kambos.

## ZARNATA CASTLE

The earliest record of Zarnata is that in 1427 it was ceded by the Byzantine ruler of Morea, Theodore, to his brother Constantine Palaiologos but there is evidence that it was inhabited as a strongpoint much earlier than this. The only remaining evidence of Byzantine occupation are some sections of Medieval wall and the Church of Agios Nikolaos in which some excellent 15th Century frescos can still be seen. Sections of ancient wall have been identified as either prehistoric or Classical (archaeologists' opinions differ again) but whichever, there may have been a Mycenaean acropolis here.

The Tower of Zarnata Castle

The next record is a Venetian reference dated 1618 to the Kastro of Zarnata as being the stronghold of a Maniat clan with 80 families living within its protection. In the Turkish-Venetian war in Crete in 1645 - 1665, the Venetians were supported by the Maniats. The Turkish victory resulted in greater Turkish control in the Mani and they rebuilt Zarnata, Kelefa and Porto Kayio castles to establish a string of defensive castles the length of the peninsula. At Zarnata they built a small fortress on the ruins of an older castle, evicted the Maniat families living there and took over a number of houses, each with its own cistern for storing water. They built a Mosque, baths and shops and in 1671 they installed a Turkish Garrison. The whole top of the hill was surrounded by an almost circular wall, 10 metres high in some places, with a raised walkway and battlements and reinforced by two round and four rectangular towers. The main gate was incorporated in a rectangular tower on the south side of the wall with another gate on the north side. The central fortress had a battery of six cannon and there were 45 other cannon on the perimeter walls.

The Venetians took control of the Mani after the Turkish-Venetian war of 1685 - 1699 and installed their own garrison at Zarnata. They compromised with the Maniats by appointing a local clan chief as Kapetanios, to administer and control the area, and so handed control of Zarnata to the Maniats. When the Turks initiated the appointment of a 'Bey' to govern the entire area of the Mani, the first Bey, Koutifaris, and the fourth Bey, Koumoundouros, both had their headquarters at Zarnata.

Today Zarnata Castle is still an imposing Fortress, visible from a long way off and dominating the area. On the top is a ruined 3 storey tower and castellated dwelling within a circular, fortified enclosure. Adjacent to this is the church of Agios Nikolaos and the frescos inside are well worth seeing. The Zodiac on the ceiling is fascinating and one of the frescos on the walls depicts some very exotic animals including elephants, camels and lions and a fierce horned monster. The Mediterranean is depicted adjacent to this with many fish and sea creatures and a splendid "Gorgona" - a two tailed mermaid. There is a "pictograph" - a story told in cartoon form - showing the creation and the fall from grace of Adam and Eve and above the carved iconostasis, a beautiful fresco of the Virgin Mary in flowing red robes. There are many other frescos too numerous to catalogue here.

The strong outer walls which encompassed the castle are still complete in many places and it is very easy to spend several hours exploring this site.

## MALTA

When you return to the road below the castle, turn left away from Stavropigio and follow the road round to the nearby village of Malta, just a few meters away. The village has many old houses and a large church (locked) with a clock tower. The only date I found was 1948, marked on concrete on a wall, but this is when it was repaired.

Some of the houses in Malta have curious conical decorations in a row along the apex of the roof. I do not know their purpose but there was a custom of putting a bottle of Holy Water on the roof to prevent lightening strikes and occasionally a stone effigy for the same reason and you can see examples of this in Malta and in some other villages. The rows of conical decorations were observed at Malta in 1810 by a German traveller with the splendid name of Otto Magnus von Stackleberg who suggested it was a custom going back to antiquity. If you want to explore Malta, then park by the church and walk round.

The road from Malta towards the main road takes you from the church and past the lone tower of Mavrikos on a hill on your right. It is possible to climb up to it by a path which runs down the side of a chain link fence at the side of the road and then weaves up the hill but it is very overgrown and thorny so wear trousers if you don't want your legs lacerated! It was built in 1814 according to the date on the Zematistra over the main door where there is also a carved head and the mouth of a cannon. There are additional stone cannon protruding below the battlements. Mavrikos is described as 'a notable of Malta'. It was obviously built for defensive purposes which is why the main door is on the first floor and could only be reached by removable wooden stairs. The ground floor is a storeroom or

Mavrikos Tower - Malta

Gouva with a vaulted ceiling and the hole in the outer wall was probably made much later when the tower no longer served a martial purpose. The only inhabitants now are a pair of Little Owls, if they are still there! The little church next to the tower was not particularly interesting.

From here it is a few hundred metres to the main road where you turn left to continue your journey south.


**THE MONASTERY OF ANDROUVENITSA**

Less than 1 kilometer from Malta, you will see a road on your left. There is a small, stone-built shrine in the shape of a temple and a signpost bearing the monastery's name. A few hundred meters along this road you reach the high, defensive wall which encloses the monastery with a large solid wooden gateway. On this gate are the times when the monastery is open to the public but, despite several attempts, I have never found it open so I see no point in publishing the opening times! Within the wall, I have read that there is a cruciform Byzantine church with an octagonal cupola and this has some 13th and 14th Century frescos preserved inside. One side of the monastery is taken up with what I assume to be the monks' quarters. (They may be Nuns' quarters as I have also seen this described as a Convent).

From the monastery, the main road continues south with fantastic views of the basin in which Kambos lies and the encircling mountains beyond. The road then goes through a wide pass and heads back towards the coast. Just after a left hand bend, you get your first view of the Mani coastline running away to the south and it is worth pausing here for a good look. Below you, you will see Kardamyli with its small harbour and the island just offshore. Further down the coast, on a clear day, you can see the akropolis of Stoupa and further away, the small peninsula that juts into the sea at Trachila. Far beyond this is the plateau of Cavo Grosso. Inland, the you will see small, scattered villages on the forward slopes of the mountains which dominate the whole panoramic view.

## PROSILIO

The road now starts a slow, winding descent to sea level and, about 6 kilometers from Stavropigio, you reach the village of Prosilio which nestles on the hillside just beside the main Kalamata road and is dominated by the large, new-looking church close to the top of the village. As you enter the little square there is a tower in ruins on the right. I have no references to the history of Prosilio at all but it is the start of the road to Tseria which is a village high in the mountains behind.

The road to Tseria is diagonally across the little square in Prosilio and from there it follows the contours for 5 kilometers above the deep Viros Gorge which runs into the sea at Kardamyli. As you get closer to Tseria you will see a Kalderimi and a small stone bridge on your right hand side. Just past here is the side road to Katafigio and Pedino.

## KATAFIGIO & PEDINO

As you approach Tseria there is a turn-off to your right with a signpost indicating both villages. They are both small, attractive villages but, as they are not individually signposted, I don't know which is which! (Katafigio means 'refuge' and is a fairly common place name, especially for caves). I'm told that there is a Kalderimi which runs from here down to Kalyves and then into the gorge and on to Kardamyli and another which runs into the gorge by way of the Monastery of Sotiros but I have never walked either of them. The walks take about an hour or so - downhill all the way.

## TSERIA

Tseria sits on the northern side of the Viros Gorge, opposite Exochori. As you enter the village the road narrows so I suggest you park and walk. The view below you to Kardamyli and the sea is stunning and there are a few tavernas here that must have the best panoramic views of any in Greece!

31

The narrow road winds through the village to a church on your left, next to a tiny square. The church is dated 1836 while the cupola on top is dated 1844. There are some wonderful carved, stone decorations on the side of the church next to the tiny square. These include some dancers and musicians, a child-like drawing of a donkey being induced to move by a 'bait' (carrot?) being dangled in front of it on a stick and, just left of and slightly above the door, the Archangel Michael who is often depicted with a sword in hand and a fierce, grotesque face on the breastplate of his armour.

Further on there is a larger, more recent (1880) church and the road then wanders on towards the edge of the gorge and some houses slightly lower down - one of which appears to be a restored tower house but I didn't get close to it. If you follow the path straight on you come to the edge of the gorge with Exochori on the opposite side. On the slope below you is a small, round sentry tower which blends so well with its surroundings that it is quite hard to see. The views from here are wonderful unless you suffer from vertigo! In early spring, if you look up the gorge, the mountains are still covered in snow and so bright in the spring sunshine that it hurts your eyes to look at them. Another Kalderimi runs from Tseria, into the gorge beyond the village and up again on the other side to Exochori but that walk is strictly for the experienced, energetic type which rules me out! It takes about one and a half to two hours to complete.

## KALYVES

From Tseria, return to the main road at Prosilio to resume the journey south. The road continues a slow descent to the coast as it follows the contours of the hillsides and the next village you reach is Kalyves, just off the main road on your left. Just after you leave the main road there is a small church on your left with a recent mosaic above the door but I think the church itself is quite old. (The church was locked).

There is a large 'car park' when you reach the hamlet and just below it is a small church among some ruined houses. The frescos here are quite badly damaged but on the wall by the door they seem to have a theme of Martyrs and include an inverted crucifiction, a decapitation (John the Baptist?) and someone tied to a wheel which appears to rotate over a fire. From outside the church there is a stunning view of Viros Gorge.

The other Church in the village (also locked) has been plastered and white washed on the outside but the bell tower has some relief decorations which can still be seen. There are only a few houses in the hamlet but the finest of these is in ruins. It was once a substantial house with a walled courtyard and access through an arched door. The entrance to the main part of the house is up some wide stone steps over a liakos to the first floor. The main door and windows are all arched marble.

# KARDAMYLI

The main road from Kalyves starts a more rapid descent to the coast with a series of sharp bends as it meanders down the mountainside to Kardamyli which is about 8 kilometers from Prosilio although the winding route makes it seem further.

Kardamyli was originally named after Kardamos, the son of Lakon who was the first king of Lakonia and it always had ties with Sparta. In Homer's Iliad, he records that this was one of the towns offered by Agamemnon to Achilles to heal the rift that he had caused by taking the captive girl Briseis from him, so it would seem to have been a recognised town in Mycenaean times. The rift between these two heroes had brought the Greek efforts against Troy to a grinding halt, Hector was causing havoc and the Trojans had driven the Greeks back to a defensive line where their ships were pulled up on the beach. Achilles was sulking in his tent and refusing to fight. He was keeping his contingent away from the fighting as well and the loss of this great hero and his fighting men had totally demoralised the Greek forces.

Pausanias recorded that there was a sacred precinct in Kardamyli which was dedicated to the Nereids, the sea nymphs, who were the fifty lovely daughters of Nereus and Doris. (Nereus was the Old Man of the Sea - The Mediterranean - and "A trusty God and gentle who thinks just and kindly thoughts and never lies" according to Hesiod. Doris was a daughter of Ocean, a Titan). Legend has it that the Nereids emerged from the sea at this spot to catch sight of Pyrrhos, the son of Achilles, as he passed on his way to Sparta to marry Hermione, the daughter of Menelaos and Helen of Troy. Achilles was the son of Thetis, one of the Nereids, so it is only natural that the Nereids would have a special interest in her grandson Pyrrhos. The site of this sanctuary is possibly occupied by the church of "The Falling Asleep of the Virgin Mary" which is the large white church in the square.

Another link between Kardamyli and the Gods is the tomb of the Dioscouri, the heavenly twins, Castor and Pollux. Their mother, Leda, was seduced by Zeus in the form of a Swan and she gave birth to an egg from which the twins hatched. Their sister was Helen of Troy. This double tomb is carved in the rock alongside the path that leads towards the acropolis from Pano Kardamyli. It is not known whose tombs these really are and Pausanias does not report on them although he usually recorded the location of important tombs and any history they may have. He does report that in the town there was "a sanctuary of Athene and a Karneian Apollo in the local Dorian style." On the acropolis above Pano Kardamyli there is evidence that this feature was used from Neolithic times until medieval times but it has never been properly excavated.

From the 1st Century BC until the 2nd Century AD, Kardamyli was the main port of Sparta. Gythio had been the main port but had joined the League of Free Lakonian Cities. Sparta was linked to Kardamyli by a path over the Taygetos Mountains and I'm told you can still follow this route if you are feeling energetic! The island just off the harbour is Meropi or Amigdaloniso with a small Venetian castle and a church dedicated to the Virgin Mary. Leake says there was a monastery there in his time.

Agios Spiridon - Old Kardamyli

The town itself is charming. The main street is flanked by old houses with several tavernas, shops and Kafeneons and there are other places to eat and drink off the main street towards the sea. At the southern end of the town is a rough road which takes you down into the harbour. It is extremely picturesque and the harbour jetty has what used to be a fortified customs house and a small church built on it. Independant travellers can usually find accommodation here without much difficulty - just ask in the tavernas and bars or look for signs which advertise rooms.

NOTE FOR WALKERS:
There are many excellant walks in this area, especially those connected with the Viros Gorge, and the Local Community have produced a free map/guide to help you. Many of the shops and tavernas have copies available and the Bookshop on the main street is also a likely place to find one.

# THE TROUPAKIS FAMILY COMPLEX - PANO KARDAMYLI

The "family complex" in Pano Kardamyli is a good example of a typical Outer Mani walled and fortified, defensive family grouping which served as a "clan" stronghold and power base. It lies to the east of the main road through the town, behind the newer houses and is well worth investigating. To reach it, walk along the narrow road which leads from the War Memorial in the small square at the north end of the main street.

The Troupakis family grew to prominence and power in Androuvitsa (Exochori) and then created the complex in Kardamyli because the harbour gave them access to the sea. The family are thought to have been refugees from Mystras when the city fell to the Turks in 1461. As fugitives, they moved to caves in the Taygetos Mountains at Androuvitsa along with many others from Mystras. The Maniats had long been accustomed to taking refuge in caves in times of trouble and there are many examples of fortified caves throughout the Peninsula. The local dialect word "Troupa" means a "hole" and this Troglodyte existence gave the Troupakis family their name.

The complex appears to have been started in the early 18th Century by 'Kapetanios' Panayotis Troupakis who had four sons; Michael, Petros, Theodorus and Yanis. As the oldest son, Michael inherited the main section of the complex by the Church of Agios Spiridon, with his brothers living in adjacent, mutually defensive properties. Michael became the second Bey of the Mani in 1779 and as well as Kardamyli, he acquired Zarnata Castle at Kambos and the defensive complex at Kitries. Kardamyli remained, however, as Michael's administrative centre, residence and main garrison. His 'reign' as Bey ended in 1782 when he was beheaded by the Sultan.

Michael's son, Kapetanios Mourtzinos Troupakis, became head of the clan and gave his name to the "Mourtzinos War Tower" which still stands in the complex. Above the door of the War Tower is the date 1808 which is when it was rebuilt following its destruction during a three month siege by a rival family, not named in my reference but in his memoirs Kolokotronis stated that Mourtzinos was banished by Antonbey. This occurred in 1805 (?) and resulted in Mourtzinos being exiled to Zakynthos for three years until given amnesty by the Turks and allowed to return to Kardamyli. Here he restored the complex and reclaimed leadership as Kapetanios. In 1813, a visiting Englishman, J.R. Cockerell gave this description of Mourtzinos and the complex.

"His castle consists of a courtyard and a church surrounded by various towers. There is a stone bench at his door where he sits surrounded by his vassals and his relations who all stand unless invited to sit. The village people bring him presents, tributes as it were, of fruit, flowers etc. On a lofty rock close by is a watch-tower where watch is kept night and day. The whole gave us the picture of feudal life new and hardly credible to a nineteenth century Englishman."

The watch tower referred to is "Petreas's" Tower which stands on a rocky hilltop south of the complex and gives an all round view of the approaches to Kardamyli, including the sea. The seaward aspect is further improved by a small watchtower above the harbour. Another reference also gives an insight into the position and power of the Kapetanios:

"He rang a large bell every midday before the meal and every evening before supper, thus publicly inviting those who were in need or those willing, to dine; and not a day passed that at least fifty to one hundred people, strangers to the family, were fed by him."

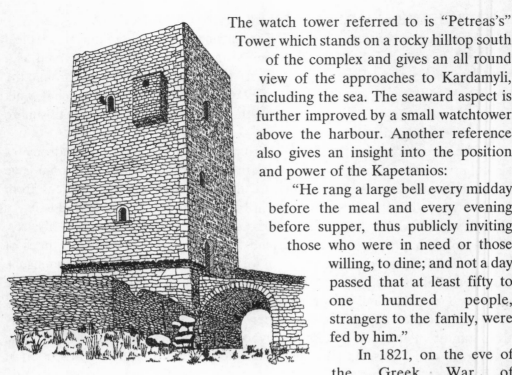

## Mourtzino's War Tower

In 1821, on the eve of the Greek War of Independence, Theodoros Kolokotronis established his headquarters at Kardamyli and here was joined by Petrobey Mavromichalis when he brought his Maniat army north from Tsimova (now Areopólis). According to local legend, they played chess in the courtyard next to the church of Agios Spiridon, using soldiers as the chess pieces on a board marked out in chalk. Kolokotronis doesn't mention this in his memoirs (maybe he lost!) and his relationship with Mavromichalis seems to have been very 'guarded' as he says, "He (Mavromichalis) behaved himself tolerably well towards me and it is not true that he betrayed me to the Turks, for he had not the power to do so even if he had the will, for besides my friendship with Mourtzinos, it is a custom in Mani to help everyone who goes there for a place of refuge." He also says, "I went to Mourtzinos as to a friend and of the same district. Mavromichalis had the title of Bey but Mourtzinos had the power in Mani." This statement is not accurate. Mourtzinos may well have held power in Exo Mani but Petrobey was the most powerful man in Mesa Mani.

From Kardamyli they marched on Kalamata and there defeated the Turkish Garrison in the first victory of the war which finally liberated Greece. To quote Kolokotronis again, "On the 23rd March we fell upon the Turks at Kalamata. They were led by Arnoutogles, a man of some importance in Tripolitsa (Tripoli). We had two thousand Maniats, with Mourtzinos and Petrobey." Mourtzinos's only son, Dionysios, also distinguished himself as a great fighter in this war and in 1830 became War Minister in the newly formed Greek Government.

## PROASTIO

South of Kardamyli, the road swings left around a wide, shallow gorge with many new houses and apartments down below on the right. On the far side of this gully, about two kilometers from Kardamyli, is a road to your left which is signposted Proastio and Exochori.

The road zig-zags up the mountainside with views along the coast to the north and south and then enters Proastio. As you approach the village, there is a kalderimi on your left, by a small church, and this takes you down the mountain side to Kardamyli. A little further on you will see a large fountain on your left but a sign warns you not to drink the water.

Proastio was one of the oldest and most important settlements in N.W. Mani according to a survey conducted in 1479. In 1618 there were 100 families living there and throughout the 17th Century it suffered from periodic attacks by the Turks. After the Turkish-Venetian War in Crete (1645 - 1665), when the Maniats had openly supported the Venetians, the Turks increased their attacks on the Mani and in 1670 they burnt Proastio as it had become an important Maniat military base.

In 1743 a record shows that Proastio was the seat of a Bishopric and this is reflected by the religious buildings - monasteries, parish and family churches - of which there are more than 30 that can be seen in the village today. The Monastery of the Sts. Theodoros can be reached by taking the Neochori-Kastania road out of Proastio. This leads off to the right just after you pass through the square with a large church to the left of the main road. On this road you pass the stone quarries and a cemetery and just further on, an old church perched slightly above the road on the left. It has two doors and in fact has two knaves, with a small internal door connecting the two. There are frescos in both but their condition is failing. On your right you will see the 19th Century tower dwelling of Patriarcheas, and you then come to a concrete road on your left which goes towards the monastery. (There is a sign but it is falling down). This concrete road turns into a rough track - so don't use a car - and the monastery is just a short walk through the olives. The monastery is dedicated to the Sts. Theodoros and was established in the 13th Century. There is a very small, ruined church with a collapsed cupola and sanctuary with fragments of frescos remaining. The other church is much larger with small buildings on either side but is usually kept locked. Between the churches are the derelict remains of the monks cells dated 1704. The area is enclosed in dry stone walls and by massive cacti.

If you go further on the Neochori road, past the turn-off for the monastery, you will come to an old stone bridge that spans a gorge with a great view straight down. Not far beyond here the road turns to track so turn back if you are in a car. If you are walking, it will take approximately two to two and a half hours to reach Saidona.

To explore the other churches and old houses in the village, park in Proastio and walk round - no matter where you go you will find churches and it would take me months to record them all in detail.

## THE ROAD TO EXOCHORI

As you leave Proastio on the Exochori road, there is a walled enclosure with a church on your left over a small gorge. The sign says Agios Yiorgos (St. George) but the track to the church is not very suitable for cars. The church has some frescos but I have yet to confirm what the enclosure was although I suspect it was another monastery. There are roofless buildings which were probably Monks cells and a large cistern (exposed - so don't fall in it) in the middle of the enclosure with high stone walls all around.

On the main road, opposite the turnoff to Agios Yiorgos, you can see the cuts and "shelves" where the rock has been quarried for limestone blocks. About 50 metres from the road (follow the track and bear slightly right) is an ancient Mycenaean Tomb. A short tunnel, the smooth sides of which taper towards the top, was cut into the rock but the roof of this tunnel has now disappeared - presumably quarried. The inverted, blunted, "V" shaped wedge above the door to the tomb shows the original height of the tunnel. The entrance to the tomb is closed by a mesh screen but you can see into the tomb chamber which is circular inside with a low walls that taper slightly towards a flat ceiling. It is not a terribly exciting site but it bears witness to an early occupation of the area.

A couple of kilometers beyond here is a small hamlet, Lakos, consisting of just a few houses to the left of the road. I saw nothing remarkable here so continue on to Exochori which is about three kilometers away.

## EXOCHORI & ANDROUVITSA

This gets a bit complicated. On one map, Exochori and Androuvitsa are separate villages. Another two maps show Exochori only and another two don't show either! On the ground, there is no obvious separation and no distinct sign for Androuvitsa. Historically, Androuvitsa and Exochori are part of one 'Chora' and a Venetian document of 1618 records them as such. This Chora was the seat of one of the local governors, the Kapetanios, as early as the 13th Century and in the 14th Century a section of this region was given to a Frankish Nobleman, Nicolas Acciaiuoli. In the 15th Century it was a fief of the Palaiologos family who were the ruling Byzantine family. During the 17th Century, the area suffered from Turkish raids as did Proastio. Leake records that the Kapetanios of Androuvitsa in 1805 was Panayotis Troupakis who governed 700 houses in the district. This suggests that the Chora extended to Kardamyli where the Troupakis family had their stronghold.

As you enter the village, the majority of buildings are on the side of the hill to the right of the road. There is a gorge on the left with a narrow road, signposted 'Kato Chora' - lower village, leading to churches and houses on the other side. Don't go this way if you are in a car! If you carry on up the road you come to a turn-off on your left - not signposted but recognisable by the new tarmac. This brings you out above the buildings at the top end of Kato Chora. There is a fantastic view across the gorge of Viros to Tseria and right up the gorge to the high mountains beyond. You can also see the kalderimi which runs from here down into the gorge and back up the other side to Tseria. If you walk down through the Kato Chora from here, there are some large churches and old houses as you make your way along narrow lanes. The churches were all locked when I was there so I cannot report on them. One had a damaged bell tower with many decorations including (quite high up) a two-masted sailing ship - a popular theme you can often see on bell towers.

If you return to the 'main road' and turn left, you come to more houses on your right and a few more above you on the left. This collection of separate house groups seems to make up the collective Chora of Androuvista. The views from all this area are wonderful. There is a sign here to the Forest of Vasiliki, Saidona etc but it really is a terrible track so don't go if you are in a car! If you decide to walk, it will take about three hours - longer if you explore the monasteries of Agios Samouli and Vaidenitsa. (see Saidona for details). If you are driving, return to the main road below Proastio.

## STOUPA

The main road continues south along the coast from the turn-off for Proastio towards Stoupa, which is about 9 kilometers from Kardamyli. It follows the rocky coastline for about two kilometres and then circles round a small inlet with a stoney beach below the road. This is popular with nude sunbathers so don't be shocked if you fancy a quick dip and go down to the beach! A little further on is another small, shingle beach and above this is the camping ground of Delphinia (Dolphin) which has also given its name to the beach.

You are now approaching Stoupa and you soon see the solitary flat-topped hill which is the akropolis of the village. Stoupa lies on the shore of a fertile coastal plain, hemmed in by the mountains rising to the east and the Bay of Messinia to the west and stretching south as far as Agios Dimitrios. Olive groves surround the village and creep up the hillsides towards the mountains in a series of terraces and produce olive oil which is second to none for flavour and fragrance. Oil production is the mainstay of the local economy and much of the oil has always been bought by Italy to boost the flavour of the comparatively bland Italian olive oil.

Stoupa was known in ancient times as Lefktra, a Free Lakonian City which declared independence from Sparta, and this name survives as Lefktron, the village immediately behind Stoupa. Pausanias called here on his travels and recorded that "Lefktra is two and a half miles from Pephnos (Agios Dimitrios). Why the city is called Lefktra I have no idea, but if it was named after Lefkippos, son of Periers, as the Messinians say, I suppose that is why the people here worship Asklepios most of the Gods, believing he was the son of Lefkippos's daughter Arsinoe. (Asklepios was a son of Apollo and was raised by Cheiron, a wise centaur, who taught him medicine and the art of healing. He became the patron of that art and was eventually worshipped as a god). There is a stone statue of Asklepios and elsewhere of Ino. (Minor goddess of the sea with the power to save sailors from shipwrecks). There is also a shrine and statue of Priam's daughter Kassandra, locally called Alexandra; and there are wooden idols of Karneian Apollo exactly according to the traditions of the Lakonians of Sparta. On the Akropolis is a sanctuary of Athena with a statue and there are a shrine and sacred wood of Love at Lefktra; in the winter water runs through the wood but even if it flooded it could never clear away all the leaves that drop from those trees in early spring. (meaning it was a large wood?). I will describe something that I know happened on the the ground near the sea at Lefktra in my own time. A wind carried fire into the wood and destroyed most of the trees; when the place was stripped bare they found a statue put up there to Zeus of Ithome. The Messinians say this is a proof that Lefktra belonged to Messinia in ancient times but it is possible that even if the Lakonians lived at Lefktra from the beginning, they could still worship Zeus of Ithome."

Clearly Stoupa was a substantial settlement, ownership of which was disputed by Lakonia and Messinia but all that survives from Pausanias' description is the acropolis, now called the Kastro (castle) after the fortress built there by William (Guillaume) de Villehardouin in 1252 following the conquest of the Peloponnese by the Franks. It was called Beaufort but very little remains to be seen except for a few walls and the remains of a tower on the summit. The castle was also called "Yisterna" which means cistern and there is a large cistern on the summit. The Museum in Kalamata displays a small, carved marble head of Athena which was found here.

From this time on, the History of Stoupa parallels that of the rest of Exo Mani. There are very few old houses in Stoupa but that is not surprising - because of attacks by the Turks and pirates, nobody would have lived so close to the sea shore and they would have concentrated further inland at Lefktron where there used to be some tower houses. In a list of Kapetani given to him by Petrobey

Mavromichalis, Leake recorded that Lefktron was the headquarters of the Christeas family who governed the area including Agios Dimitrios and Platsa. Stoupa itself would not have developed until after the Greek War of Independence when it would be deemed safer to live on the shore and even now it is little more than a village because the population during the winter is very small compared to summer.

Stoupa is the main tourist resort for the area because of its wonderful beaches and a small harbour patrolled by the resident ducks who cruise around in "line-astern" in the hope of a crust of bread. At the same time, it has managed to maintain its character as a village or small town, albeit a modern one in terms of the majority of the buildings. It is a quiet resort - no Karaoke, Discos etc!! - and the tavernas still specialise in traditional Greek dishes. The most common remark I hear from visitors is that it reminds them of Greece and the islands of twenty to thirty years ago. If you travel here independently, as opposed to package tour, you can usually find accommodation although this could be a problem in July and August when the resort fills with Athenians escaping the oppressive heat and polution of that blighted city.

There is also another camping ground, Kalogria, at the north end of the village, above the beautiful beach of the same name. It is hard to imagine now, but Kalogria was where the local goatherds used to drive their flocks into the sea to wash them - a sort of salt-water sheep-dip!

NOTES FOR WALKERS. There are several great walks in the area, especially to and from the mountain villages behind Stoupa, and there is a booklet and map to guide you which is sold by the tour operators from their respective offices.

## NEOCHORI

The road to Neochori takes you up through the olive groves to the hills behind Stoupa. The large white building you pass is a modern olive oil bottling plant and there is a wonderful view of Stoupa, Agios Nikolaos and Agios Dimitrios from here. Neochori is part of the Chora of Lefktron, as is Pyrgos above.

When you get to Neochori you cannot drive very far into the village because the streets are narrow, so park and walk round. There are many old houses, some of which are derelict, and one or two with small towers. If you bear left (north) you will find an old, derelict olive press with two massive stone wheels used for crushing the olives. There is also find a single, massive stone wheel in a little square which was also once a mill and apparently turned by a donkey or mule. This one appears more suitable for grain. There is a large, modern church with a tall bell tower in the centre of the village with a war memorial and cannon in the grounds.

The road climbs higher as you leave Neochori towards Pyrgos, 4 kilometers away, and there is a ruined tower and houses on your left above the road. If you park close to here and take the dirt road running off to your right  you come across a 'fortified' cave with an arched door protected by a Zematistra.  A little further on there is a small church. There are more caves above the road to the left of the ruined tower house. These are also walled and in some of them you can see how they were arranged for human occupation and one or two include their own water cisterns. They are mainly used now for goats but their original purpose as human habitations is clear to see.

## PYRGOS

Pyrgos itself stands on the edge of a plateau with wonderful views of the coastline and olive groves below and the mountains behind. Don't try to drive into the village itself but there is a "Parkin" area by the main road so leave your car there. It is a charming village with several churches and it is worth walking round the narrow, twisting alleys many of which have been decorated with white-wash in  swirling, floral  designs.

Pyrgos was captured by the Turks in 1481 during their occupation of Messinian Mani after the Venetian-Turkish War 1463 - 1479 and at the same time they occupied Kastania and fortified it. Just outside the village is an olive press where they specialise in processing 'Organic' olives that have not been treated with chemical fertilisers and sprays and you can buy their oil and olives here, as well as other organic produce.

## KASTANIA

The road runs north from Pyrgos for 5 kilometers until you reach Kastania, which  is a 'classic example' of an Exo-Mani mountain village. It is completely invisible from the coast below and is tucked defensively into the top of a small gorge at the head of which is a spring and fountain. This position made a coastal raid less likely -  the approach roads and village easier to defend -  provided a sheltered escape route up the gorge behind if needed -  and an ample water supply.

The village is protected by a tower house, in a reasonable state of repair, and narrow, twisting lanes wind upwards among the old houses, many of which still have their original 'tikles' roofs. You will also find several old churches with frescos in various states of repair. It is a beautiful village and worth taking the time to explore.

Kastania was important as it was headquarters for one of the regional Kapetanios, Konstantinos Dourakis, and it is his 5 storey tower house which still dominates the village. Theodoros Kolokotronis took refuge here during the persecution of the Klephts in 1803 "to my old friend Captain Konstantes

Douraki, whom I trusted greatly because I had taken care of his family in former times, and because he was, as it were, my co-father-in-law, for I had betrothed my daughter to his son"." Never-the-less, his friend planned to betray him for 'grosia' (money). "Douraki, when he looked upon the grosia, determined to betray me for the Maniats will do anything for grosia".

Dourakis put opium in his wine but Kolokotronis was warned and knocked it over. He then announced his intention to leave. "He tried to persuade me to go into his house and take wine with him before I left and went in to prepare it and at the same time he ordered some men to fall upon me and secure me whilst we were drinking together, but his brother prevented me from going in and he also kept the dogs from barking whilst we got away." He then escaped, aided by Dourakis's brother, and fled to Kastanitsa on the other side of the mountains.

The church next to the tower has been rendered in concrete outside and plastered inside and a rather ugly concrete superstructure added which serves as a bell tower.

Dourakis's War Tower

However, closer examination inside shows that this church is older than it now looks and there are particularly fine carved marbles in the templon, especially over the entrance to the sanctuary. The carved marble capitals atop the two pillars have been painted but depict animals and what appear to be horsemen. I cannot help but wonder what lies beneath all the interior plaster! There is also a "Gynaikonitis" - a gallery at the rear of the church which was reserved for women. On the outside, the carved marble around the door appears to be from an old templon and the spouts on the cupola seem to be from a much older church - which again suggests that an old church is masquerading as a much newer building.

Higher up the village is the old church of Agios Petros with beautiful cloisonné brickwork decoration and old 'tikles' roof-tiles. Above one window in the southern wall is a semi-circle of marble with a carved eagle holding a snake in its talons and the cupola has faces carved on some of the spouts which protrude from it almost like gargoyles.

The church was originally much smaller than it now appears and you can see that the narthex has been added on and then the bell tower built on to the narthex, creating a new doorway into the church. Inside the narthex, the roof is domed although the exterior is a pitched tikles roof. It may well be that this was originally domed like the 11th Century churches of Agios Sotiras at Gardenitsa and St. Michaels at Boulari but I have read that these two were the only churches with this feature in Mani. I think this church was probably the same, especially as it has a double arch in the south wall - very similar again to the church at Gardenitsa - but has been altered at a later date.

Above the door into the church itself is a carved marble showing a griffin attacking an animal, possibly a deer, and two large birds which might be peacocks. Inside the church, the marble capitals on the columns and the marble of the templon are equally beautifuly carved but the frescos are badly damaged by soot and what appears to be salt seeping from the plaster. There is also a ring of carved marble around the base of the dome of the cupola. A local told me the church was 950 years old although serious attempts to date it have failed, but it is probably early Byzantine. The bell tower is dated 1813 and has some interesting decorations and designs including two small stone heads.

The small, cruciform church on the left as you enter the village has some beautiful cloisonné decorations on the outside. The frescos inside are in poor condition but there is a wonderful, sad-looking face of Christ looking down from an arch. On the north wall is a naked Christ covered in thin wavy blue lines as though suggesting he is immersed up to his neck in water. The rest of the fresco is damaged and it may depict his baptism in the River Jordan but the work is crude and naive compared to the other pictures. This church is also thought to be early Byzantine but again has not been dated.

## SAIDONA

The road continues towards Saidona which is about 8 kilometers further north and, shortly after leaving Kastania, there is a very small vaulted church on your right but the frescos have been whitewashed so there is very little to see inside.

Saidona is the village you can see perched high in the mountains north of Stoupa and at night the lights from here seem to be suspended in the sky. As you enter Saidona, there is a war memorial on the right which includes a plaque to the casualties of the Greek Civil War and another is dedicated to those killed when a force of Italians set fire to the gorge below Saidona and destroyed much of the village. The 'castle-like' building right at the top of the village is only about fifteen years old although parts of it are much older. It is difficult to park in Saidona without causing an obstruction so if you want to explore, park just outside and walk round.

It is possible in a 4x4 or on foot, to travel beyond Saidona on a rough road to Exochori. There are two deserted monasteries on this route but they are not easy to see from the road. The first, the Monastery of Agios Samouli, is above the road on your right as you travel from Saidona and you just glimpse it through the trees where the road does a sharp left turn and follows the contour round a small gorge. The monastery is protected by a defensive wall and a tower and is just a short walk up the hill through the brush.

The second monastery, Vaidenitsa, is further on and again is situated where the road follows the contour into a small gorge. As you approach the area, you will see the tower of Kitriniaris, beside the road on the opposite side of the gorge, perched on an outcrop of rock. The monastery cannot be seen from the road but a path which is easy to follow takes you up the gorge, shaded by wonderful walnut trees.

In the spring it is over-run with wild flowers and orchids and the mountain stream gurgles among the rocks in the gorge and sparkles in the patches of sunlight that penetrate the canopy of the massive trees. It is a magical, peaceful place - so much so that I was reluctant to include it in this book for purely selfish reasons. This monastery was also protected by a tower but it and the house in which the monks lived were burned by the Italians during the war. The church, which has been restored, sits on an outcrop of rock with a high defensive wall protecting the courtyard and entrance and, above this, the tower keeps a silent vigil. It is a beautiful setting and well worth visiting.

The tower of Kitriniaris, which is on the far side of the gorge towards Exochori, is one of my favourites and it seems to melt like a candle onto the rocky outcrop on which it stands. Kolokotronis was involved here in a feud in support of the Dourakis family from Kastania. "Kaptain Konstantine Douraki, who had been a friend of my father, had begun a feud about this time with Kitriniari, and we sent him reinforcements. The Maniotes had caused him (Kitriniaris) to be in great straits, and he therefore desired to deliver the place up, and asked for me. His design, however, was not to surrender, but to kill me if possible by an act of treachery. He came himself outside the gate of the tower in order to surrender it, but he had placed some men inside, and these men discharged six guns full at me. I was struck, but not hurt; I fell down under the roof of the tower gate, and my own men thinking that they had killed me, wanted to slay the relations of Kitriniares; others however called out, 'No, let us look after Theodoros.' The brother of Kitriniares came up, and I took him by the shoulder and protected him, and at night I threw fire into the tower, and it was then delivered up." Kolokotronis was then asked if he intended to kill those who had betrayed him and he replied, "God has preserved me, so I grant them their lives." This incident makes the subsequent betrayal of Kolokotronis by Dourakis at Kastania even more incomprehensible!

## KARIOVOUNI

The road which leads to Kariovouni and then on to Milia is between Pyrgos and Kastania, so you need to backtrack from Saidona and turn left where you see the relevant signpost. The road runs for 6 kilometers above the gorge behind Riglia and Isnia, passes through a tiny hamlet of a few houses and then reaches Kariovouni, which is tucked away, almost out of sight, at the top of a gorge. The name comes from the Greek for walnut and there is a large walnut tree on the terrace by the stream just below the road. There is a restored tower dwelling in the village and the remains of another. It is also known locally as Arachova which is a much older name and was also sometimes used to describe a Chora which included Kastania and Milia.

## MILIA

The road carries on for 5 kilometers to Milia which is an old village split into three sections - a lower section below the road, a middle section slightly further on and an upper section on a hill above. This village "and its dependencies containing 200 houses" was listed by Col. Leake as being governed by Kapetanios Kyvelaki and he also quotes the poet, Nikitas Nifakos as describing Milia thus - "From hence (Arachova) lets us proceed, by the wolf-path, to the robbers of kids and goats, the walkers at night, and record the name of the town of the kid-eating rogues, the mule-stealers, the goat-slayers, the thrice-apostate Milia, from which Garbelea is one quarter of an hour distant." Clearly, the poet was not enamoured of Milia!

The church in the small square in the lower section has a bell tower dated 1776 decorated with carvings and with a wonderful device of connecting metal rods for ringing the church bells. There is a tower house here with 'restored' concrete battlements.

In the square of the middle section is another church with a high bell tower with engravings. Looking from here due east into the mountains you can see a large building high on a ridge. This is the monastery of Panagia Giatrissa and, as a Greek friend remarked, it looks as though it would be more at home in the mountains of Tibet! If you enjoy walking, the trek to the monastery is wonderful and you will be rewarded with stunning views of the other side of the Taygetos range. There are several other churches and many old houses here and in the upper section on the hill above. The village is a sleepy, peaceful place to visit and, as is usual in these mountains, the views all round are wonderful.

When Kolokotronis was a young teenager, he lived here "In Melia in the Mani" with his uncle, following the death of his father Kostantes. "...my father was wounded by a sword thrust and afterwards killed through the treachery of a Turkish friend. His head was never recovered." The body was found three years later (recognised by an old sabre wound to his hand) and he was "interred again at Melia." His father was only 33 when he was killed but "...before he was slain he had killed with his own hand seven hundred Turkish irregulars." Kostantes and his friend Venetsanakos had become the scourge of the Turks who occupied the Bardounia area on the east side of the mountains from Milia and in 1780 were beseiged in a tower there. They refused to submit to the Turkish General Hasan Tzelaidin and they were killed in this engagement. (See Bardounia section - Mikri Kastania).

The grave of Kostantes is in fact at Garbelia which you can reach from the square in Milia, although the road is a bit rough in places. If you do go there you will see an imposing fortified house and should take the road which branches to the right. This takes you to the other end of the village where you will see a small white church which has been 'restored'. As you enter the graveyard there is a strange cave-like construction in stone against the side of the church on your right and this is Kostantes's grave, I am told, but there is no marker or dedication. The ages on the other markers in the graveyard show an amazing number of one family who lived to reach their late 90's.

A new road is being built from Milia to Platsa but at the time of writing (January 1998) it is not yet finished. When it is it will give much better access to Garbelia.

## AGIOS NIKOLAOS

This is a pleasant fishing village about 4 kms south of Stoupa and is often referred to locally as 'Selinitsa' which was its former Slavic name. It is an enjoyable place to stop and have a drink at a Kafeneon to watch the fishing boats coming and going or for an evening meal by the harbour or on the headland which protects it, but there is little of historical interest. Pausanias makes no mention of any settlement here, nor does a report by R. Hope Simpson at the British School at Athens, although there were Mycenaean settlements to the north and south at Stoupa and Agios Dimitrios.

The oval tower perched on a rock that you pass on your way into the village from the north is a remnant of the Greek Civil War - as are a couple of round, stone towers elsewhere in the village. There is a pharmacy and a post office by the harbour and accommodation is usually not difficult to find although it can become scarce in July and August. There is a coastal path between Stoupa and

Agios Nikolaos with olive groves on one side and the rocky coastline on the other and it is a pleasant stroll of about one hour between the villages.

There is no beach as such at the village but a short distance to the south (a ten minute walk from the harbour) there is a pleasant though slightly stony beach fringed by shady trees. It is very beautiful but is sometimes spoilt by camper vans which ignore the law and set up residence here.

## AGIOS DIMITRIOS

Agios Dimitrios is a small village with a little harbour which was the anchorage for Kapetanios Christeas of Stoupa and Platsa. The harbour was protected by the tower which formed part of a small complex on the headland above. In 1795, J.B.S. Morrit, a traveller, wrote "The tower of Capitano Christea was a small distance from the port and adjoining it were outbuildings and a long hall of entertainment. We dined with the family at 12 o'clock and after dinner went to the great room of the castle. In it, and on the green before it, we found near a hundred people assembled and partaking of the chief's hospitality."

Morrit also identifies this as the site that Pausanias called Pephnos where "There is a little isle off shore no bigger than a big rock....The people of Thalamai say this is where the Dioscouri were born... On this little island there are bronze statues of the Dioscouri a foot high standing on the island in the open air. When the sea sweeps over the rock in winter it never moves them. This is a wonderful thing, and also the ants here have a whiter colour than is usual." (For Dioscouri - see Kardamyli). It is pleasant to see that Pausanias was also interested in the flora and fauna of different places and in his old age, he became a keen bird-watcher. Some of the plants he recorded have never been identified and may have died out during the last two thousand years.

A report by R. Hope Simpson confirms the site of Pephnos and adds that it was a small Mycenaean settlement with further traces of ancient habitation including burials of the Roman period in this general area. I have not located these burial sites.

## SOUTH TO TRACHILA

South from Agios Dimitrios, towards Trachila, the road follows the coast with cliffs above and below you. At one place, above you but quite difficult to find, you can see the 'window' of a cave half way up the cliff face. On either side of it you can see the remains of other small stone walls. I am told a monk used to live there but how on earth he got to it I have no idea. He was 'fed and watered' by lowering a basket which was filled by local people. There are other walled caves along here but this is the most intriguing. If you are interested in Ornithology, this stretch of road is a popular haunt of hawks or falcons and the occasional buzzard, as well as Blue Rock Thrush, Nuthatches and many other small birds.

## TRACHILA

Trachila is a very attractive village tucked into the the shelter of a small headland and it is quite likely to have been the port for ancient Thalamai although Pausanias does not say so. Large old houses front onto a 'promenade' below which is the little harbour protected by a restored tower dwelling. There are a couple of cosy tavernas and a sleepy, relaxed atmosphere, so it is a place to go to 'get away from it all'.

There is a ruined tower and some derelict houses on the headland and these formed a small defensive complex. So far, I have been unable to find any details about them but they seem to pre-date the village itself.

Some maps show a road beyond Trachila - it is not there!!. Don't be surprised if you are 'ambushed' by a local lady as you enter the village. She has a small taverna on the right and will flag you down in an effort to persuade you to stop for a drink or a meal and also offer local honey or pickles for you to buy. You have to return to Agios Dimitrios from Trachila as there is no other road.

## RIGLIA

Traveling south on the main road from Stoupa, just past the turn off for Agios Nikolaos, on the left hand side, is the turn-off for Riglia. The village is in two sections with Ano Riglia just beyond the first village. Driving straight up through the village, there is a little white-washed church on your right. Unfortunately, the inside has been white-washed too but some frescos remain. Higher up, as you leave the village, is another little church with a small bell tower in a walked garden on your left. This is dated 1823 and has a remarkable marble carving above the door showing the crucifiction above a skull - a common theme which presumably represents Golgotha - "The Place of the Skull".

## ISNIA

To reach Isnia, you keep going inland above Ano Riglia but be warned - the road is narrow and 'broken up' in places with the risk of a puncture. The village itself is remarkable because the top of the village is perched on a high rock alongside the gorge which runs down from the area of Kariovouni. The scenery is wonderful and it is a good area for those who like to do some walking, especially in spring and early summer. Return to the main road by the same route.

## PIGI

Continue south on the main road which now starts to climb up into the mountains again. Pigi is a small village just off the main road before you reach Platsa, about 10 kilometers south of Stoupa. The name means Fountain or Spring and the village is tucked into the apex of a gorge which runs down the mountains to the area of Agios Dimitrios. There is a narrow lane which leads down to a small cleared area next to a derelict house and you should park there. You then walk along a narrow winding lane through the village to a small square where there is a surprisingly large church and a taverna.

The church is quite new but has a wonderful carved iconostasis. The taverna (at the time of writing) is no longer in use which is tragic because it was probably my favourite taverna in the whole area.

A track leads up from behind this church to a small white-washed church dated 1788. It has frescos including a faded but detailed fresco of the Crucifiction above the inside of the doorway. There is another small church below this one but it has been whitewashed inside.

## PLATSA

Platsa is about 2 kilometers beyond Pigi and was a stronghold of Kapetanios Christeas. Agios Dimitrios on the coast below was its harbour - protected by the Tower built there by the Christeas family. There are no dominant towers in Platsa but it is easy to see that the old houses were built with defence in mind and Platsa was attacked by the Turks several times during the 17th century. There is a large church in the main square which is flanked by large 'neo-classic' houses. Down below the church (on the left of the square as you look towards the sea) is a small church dated 1774 (locked).

If you take the narrow lane on the right of the square you come to a very small whitewashed church. This has some frescos inside, some of which are badly damaged. Further down the little lane there is another church on your left in a walled garden. This is dated 1828 but has been 'restored' inside. Below here is the Kalderimi that leads down to Agios Dimitrios.

On the southern outskirts of Platsa, just off the main road, is the church of Agios Nikolaos - Kabinari. It sits on a promontory in a beautiful setting with a small stand of pine trees overlooking the sea and is one of the oldest surviving churches in the Mani. Originally built in the 9th or 10th century with three naves and no transept, the cupola and surrounding wall and buildings were added later. It is only possible to see inside when special services are held, otherwise it is kept locked.

## NOMITSI

There are a number of churches and old houses, many of which are derelict, in Nomitsi. The first church is on the left on the outskirts but not worth visiting. The next is on the left, on a rise behind a white wall. The belfry has a date 1837 although I'm sure  the church is older. It has some frescos of which some appear to be older than others but I'm not an expert. There is a carved marble slab depicting the double-headed eagle of Byzantium set in the floor.

From the main road you will see, to the east, a large, modern looking church set back in the village. I know nothing about it and it was locked but I have the impression that under the 'modern' facade of concrete there is an old church concealed. There is also a small private church here, the roof of which protrudes into the small square. Moving on from here through the village, there is a curious church built over an old fountain but this has been renovated inside. The large stone troughs by the fountain were for washing clothes and watering animals.

Derelict Church with Bat Colony

Back on the main road, there is a small church on your right in very poor condition but with a few remaining damaged frescos and a bat colony living in the cupola. Past here on your left, on the edge of the road, is another old church with a tiny door. This too has suffered badly from the weather and neglect but a new door and windows have been put in to protect it.

Further along the main road (left), on a rise, is an old church dated 1696 but it appears to be private and the gate of the small courtyard was locked. Another small church on your left above the road has been whitewashed inside but the next on your left, just on the edge of the village is a little gem - the 11th century Church of the Metamorphosis. There are some wonderful frescos (which desperately need preservation) and a carved marble arch which spans the central door of the templon. There are also some carvings on the marble capitals of the pillars in the transept which include birds about to peck at bunches of grapes and two animals (dogs?) tied to a tree.

# THALAMES

Almost as soon as you leave Nomitsi, you are in Thalames. Pausanias records Thalames as being one of the Free Lakonian Cities where there was a sanctuary and an oracle of Ino. "The oracles are given in sleep: whatever people ask to be told, the goddess reveals it to them in dreams. There are bronze statues in the sanctuary in the open air, one of Pasiphae, the other of the Sun. It is impossible to get a clear look at the statue in the temple itself because of the wreaths, but they say it is made of bronze like the others. Fresh drinking water runs from a sacred water-spring; Pasiphae is a title of the Moon, not a local divinity of Thalamai."

Plutarch also recorded this sanctuary but said it was Pasiphae's sanctuary and oracle - not Ino's. Ino was a goddess of the sea and saved Odysseus from drowning when his raft was shattered by a storm sent by Poseidon. The Moon was also known as Phoebe or Selene and was the sister of Helios, the sun-god. The site of the "Sacred Water Spring" is thought to have been the "Jew's Well" in the square on the main road at Svina which is the southern end of Thalames. Here you can see a covered fountain just below a taverna and 50 metres north of the fountain, just below the school, is the well.

The fountain below the taverna had a series of inscribed and ornamented classical, marble stones built into the facade of the arch which covers it but in 1996 two of these marbles were stolen and now the rest have been removed for safe keeping. Next to the fountain is the pedestal of a statue and the inscription is a dedication to the Roman Emperor Marcus Aurelius.

The ancient city of Thalames is thought to have stood north east of the Jew's Well, on the high ground behind the school. There is another old well here and 50 metres to the northeast of this is the possible site of the Temple of the Goddess, tentatively identified by some Hellenic masonry (which, as usual, I cannot find!).

There is a small Byzantine Church on the hillside here which is similar in size and construction to the Metamorphosis church at Nomitsi and some frescos remain. A local told me the church is dedicated to St. Spiridon and dated to the 14th Century. I am curious about it, however, because it is not oriented with the altar facing due east and because there are several icons here to Profitas Illias - the prophet Elijah. He is normally associated with churches on mountain peaks because he has replaced Helios, the sun god. There are one or two pieces of whitewashed marble here which may be much older and I cannot help but wonder if this church is the site of something much older. It is certainly in the reported area of the old city of Thalames.

The 'Mani Museum' is here in Thalames (opposite the school) and is a strange, private collection of miscellaneous bric-a-brac including agricultural and domestic implements, prints, a few weapons, church artifacts and more. There are some old defensive houses and towers in the village, many of which are derelict, and a couple of restored tower dwellings.

## LAGADA

Two kilometers beyond Thalames is Lagada. This is a fascinating village which, unlike most of the Exo Mani villages, was divided into Family or Clan areas like the villages of Inner Mani further south. Lagada had three main divisions. The Bloutsos family were centred in 65 houses around the main square with the beautiful church of Agios Sotiras. The area around the Kapitsinos War Tower in the south of the village consisted of a further Tower dwelling (only half of which remains), a round tower and 90 houses belonging to four allied families. Above this was the Tsicholianika area with twenty houses and a church.

Agios Sotiris - Lagada

The old houses are obviously built with defence in mind and walking through the narrow lanes is fascinating. There is a ruined church on the hill above the road as you approach the square from the north. Some frescos remain and there is a very well constructed Kalderimi leading off to the north towards Thalames.

The main square of the village is dominated by the church of Agios Sotiras, which I'm told is probably 10th or 11th Century. It used to be encased in concrete and plaster but this was removed in the mid 1980's to reveal stonework decorated with the most wonderful cloisonné brickwork, especially on the belfry. The inside of the church has also been plastered over but tentative exploration has revealed some frescos beneath this. There is still a great deal of work to be done to expose these frescos once again and there is a written appeal and collection box for donations to carry on and complete this task. Please give generously!

On the road leaving Lagada to the south is a taverna by the road side. Stop just before you get to it and look to your right at the solid looking, derelict house below the road. On the wall you will see some wonderful relief decorations which include the builder in his 'top hat', monocle and splendid moustache; his wife who is, by comparison, very plain with a kerchief on her head; decorated door and window lintels; doves and a representation of Aphrodite higher up. There is also a plaque with the sun and moon and the date 1859.

The taverna is run by a splendid character called Petros and although the inside is 'basic', the food is wonderful. If you eat there in the evening, Petros can sometimes be persuaded to produce his Bazouki and play for you.

## AGIOS NIKON

From Langada the road follows the contours around a gorge and on the coast below you can see Trachila, protected by the small headland jutting out into the sea. Approximately 5 kilometers from Langada is the village of Agios Nikon.

The village is named after Saint Nikon the Repenter - the soldier, monk and missionary who is credited with converting much of the Mani to Christianity. I have also seen him referred to as Osios (The Holy) Nikon which is a title usually applied to revered men such as Hermits but who have not been canonized. This village is typical of the area and has many old houses but I have found nothing exceptional. Maybe I need to explore further. The Church in the little square on the main road, next to the war memorial, is dated 1880 and has some frescos inside.

## CHOTASIA

Approximately 3 kilometers south of Agios Nikon you will see a large map on a sign board on the right hand side of the road, adjacent to a minor road leading off to the west. This map marks the border between Messinia and Lakonia (which is why the double white lines suddenly stop here!) and the road to the right leads down to Chotasia which is a collection of houses, many of them recently built, close to the rocky shore. There is a sign advertising the 'beach' but access is by un-mettled road down a $45^{\circ}$ slope to a rocky shore and not worth the 'angst' of the descent!

There is, however, an old war tower on a rock which you pass on your way down to the village. The lower door is to a storage area and the upper door, with access to the rest of the tower, could only be reached by ladder.

## OITYLO

Continuing south for 5 kilometers from the Lakonia/Messinia border, you reach Oitylo. Pausanias records Oitylo as one of the Free Lakonian Cities and it was also recorded by Homer that Oitylo sent ships to support Agamemnon at Troy, so it has been a recognised settlement for a long time. "The sanctuary of Sarapis and the wooden idol of Kareian Apollo in the market place are worth seeing." was the only physical reference Pausanias made. It is suggested that at this time, the majority of the city was below the ridge on the lower slopes above the sea with only an acropolis where the modern town lies.

Oitylo was always an important town, strategically because it linked North and South Mani and commercially through trade, piracy and a very profitable slave trade. It was the 'capital' of the Mani before the rise to prominence of Tsimova (Areopolis) and Limeni, so it was a focus of attention for Turkish control of the area and Kelefa Castle, across the gorge, became a major garrison during the brief periods of occupation.

The constant attacks of Turkish forces during the late 17th Century and some desperate family feuds caused a mass migration from the Mani which included 1,700 people from Oitylo and Kelefa village. One migration is commemorated on a plaque in the small market place - flanked by two ancient columns which presumably came from the sanctuary referred to by Pausanias. (Patrick Leigh Fermor gives very detailed information on these migrations and the settlements they established in Tuscany and Corsica in his book, "Mani"). Most of Oitylo's towers have been destroyed but the strongly fortified houses illustrate the constant defence put up by the local inhabitants.

A narrow road leads down the cliff from the square to the Monastery of Dekoulou or you can reach it by another track which leads off the main road as it winds down into the Bay of Oitylo. There is a new house on the west end of the monastery and this family have the key to the church. Inside the church, every inch of wall is covered in frescos with parades of Saints and pictographs showing various Old and New Testament stories. There is a very ornate iconostasis, although it is damaged in some places, and this supports some lovely icons. The interior of the church is very dark so if you plan to visit, you should take a good torch or most of the frescos will be impossible to see, especially up in the dome and at the rear of the church.

Much of the village seems to be in decay and one derelict house near the 'town hall' has bits of classical marble included in its construction. Leake noted in his journal that he was unable to visit Oitylo because he was travelling under the protection of Antonbey who was allied to the Mavromichalis family by marriage. The rivalry between Tsimova and Oitylo made it unsafe for him to set foot in the town where Antonbey's protection did not apply!

## TSIGOU MONASTERY, KRIONERI, KAREA AND GERMA

As you enter Oitylo, the road branches left and a sign directs you to Gythio, via the villages of Krioneri, Karea and Germa. The road is a bit broken up in places and takes you on a loop which joins the Areopolis - Gythio road. Below a sharp right hand bend on this road, not far from Oitylo, is a good example of an old Kalderemi bridge with the path itself meandering up the hillside.

Shortly after this, a track leads off to your left (North) and follows the eastern side of a wide gorge. It starts off paved but soon deteriorates into a track which is really only suitable for a 4x4. If you follow this track you eventually reach the Monastery of Tsigou, perched on an overhanging rock on the mountain slopes. A defensive wall with many Doufekotrypes (firing loops) encloses the church and buildings and a square tower protects the eastern corner of the complex. A track takes you to the main entrance gate which is locked but the adjacent wall has collapsed allowing entry. A very unusual feature is the remains of a round tower which protected this gateway. The templon in the church has some damaged frescos while bits of others are visible where the plaster/whitewash covering has flaked away. (Another worthwhile restoration project?). The tower has been restored and looks as though it is sometimes occupied but the other monastic buildings are derelict. The view south from here is quite stunning and you can see right down the gorge and across Kelefa to the mountains above Areopolis.

The main road continues round a large 'basin' until it meets the road to Gythio. At Germa, just before the Gythio road, there is a small, Byzantine church by the roadside. I have not found a keyholder but I'm desperate to have a look inside!

## OITYLO TO AREOPOLIS

On the road down to Oitylo Bay, just on the edge of town, there is a viewing platform, with a "Kantina" in summertime, and from here you can enjoy the wonderful panorama across the Bay of Oitylo and of Kelefa Castle on the opposite side of the gorge.

## KELEFA CASTLE

You can get to Kelefa Castle by walking down into the gorge from Oitylo and then back up the other side - or if you want to drive - by taking the road to Gythio from Areopolis and turning left on the road to Kelefa village. Park on the side of the road before the village and walk across the 'heath' or drive into the village and walk from there. The village itself is worth a 'ramble' with several old churches and houses.

The castle was built by the Turks in 1670 after they had defeated the Venetians in Crete and turned their attention on the Mani and Oitylo. It is a large rectangular enclosure with high walls and bastions on the corners and could hold a garrison of 500 men. It gave the Turks a commanding view of Oitylo while dominating the harbour on the coast below and formed part of the chain of castles from Zarnata to Porto Kayio. The castle was captured by a Maniat and Venetian force in 1685 and repulsed an attempt by the Turks to regain it during the following year. They (the Turks) finally re-captured it in 1715 and rebuilt it but I cannot find any reference to how long they then occupied it. Much of the thick, curtain wall survives with three round towers on the western side facing towards the sea. The southern wall still has the parapet and battlements from which the Turks kept an eye on Oitylo and from which they could bombard the town with cannon. The interior of the castle is very overgrown in places and the undergrowth conceals the walls of various buildings within. The buildings you can see have been preserved because they contain cisterns which can still be used to provide water for grazing stock.

## KARAVOSTASI and NEO OITYLO

Driving south from Oitylo you drop down to the bay and the old harbour of Karavostasi which literally means 'ship stop'. There is little to see here although one derelict old house by the modern harbour has incorporated two small columns as door supports and these may originally have belonged to a classical building. Further along the bay is Neo Oitylo and there is very little to see here except some old houses. There are several small hotels and pensions in this area if you want to break your journey.

As I mentioned previously, this area below Oitylo is possibly the site of the ancient city and the ruins of a temple were found near the start of the gorge which divides Oitylo from Kelefa but I can find no trace of it now.

## LIMENI

Limeni was the harbour for Areopolis and strategically important for that reason. The Mavromichalis family grew to prominence in this area and, under their control, Areopolis and Limeni became the main town and main harbour of the inner Mani - often in dispute with Oitylo and its harbour, Karavostasi. The harbour was protected by a round tower (disappeared), several fortified caves, defensively built houses and the tower house of the Mavromichalis family, which is now a museum. There was also a small convent here, now derelict, but some of the frescos are still visible in the chapel which has no roof. The Russian attempt to help the Greeks overcome the Turks in 1770, The Orlov Event, started with a landing here. The expedition was a disaster.

When Leake visited here as a guest of the Mavromichalis family, the convent was still in use and he commented that it had "a little garden about it". Petrobey Mavromichalis is buried in the small church on the north shore of the harbour where there is a monument and bust over his tomb.

Leake stayed as a guest of Petros Mavromichalis before he became the Bey and wrote that he was "a smart looking man of between thirty and forty, dressed in green velvet and the genteelest Maniat I have yet seen." He told Leake the story of how, in 1792, his father rescued a British ship in distress near Pyrgos Dirou and piloted them back to Limeni with a small vessel. He then mounted a guard over the ship to prevent any attack or looting and protected the ship until it sailed again nineteen days later! A most unusual result for a ship which fell into Maniat hands!

From here the road climbs up out of the bay and past a new hotel which has been designed to look like a Mani Village. At the moment, it looks a bit raw but when the stonework has mellowed, I hope it will blend more harmoniously with the environment. It certainly has a magnificent view of the bay and I'm told by an acquaintance from Iceland that it is a very comfortable place to stay.

Fortified Cave - Limeni

## AREOPOLIS

As the crow flies, Areopolis is not far from Oitylo but the drive down into the bay and back up to the ridge on the south side is about 11 kilometers. This town links the East-West road to Gythio with the North-South road from Kalamata to the southern tip of the peninsula. As you approach the town there is a high mountain which dominates it to the east and you can see a small white building perched right on the summit. This is a church dedicated to the Prophet Elijah. (I have not been there!).

Areopolis was formerly called Tsimova but the name was changed on the 17th March, 1821 when the Maniats, led by Petrobey, left the town to march north to Kardamyli on the eve of the War of Independence. The new name is derived from Ares, the God of War, and was changed to honour the Maniats and their leader. It proved to be most appropriate as Petrobey Mavromichalis took part in - and survived - more than forty battles against the Turks. (Some sources say the name was changed after the War of Independence - not on the 17th March 1821).

There is a statue of Petrobey, holding a large sword, in the main square which is surrounded by cafes and restaurants. Do not be put off by the modern buildings in this area - the old part of Areopolis is delightful, as befits its history and heritage. To reach it, walk down from the north of the square (the side which Petrobey's statue is facing) towards the west (the sea), and you will come to a small square with a large church with a very impressive campanile on the south side. This is the square where the flag of revolution was first unfurled and a plaque on the wall commemorates the event.

The church is Taxiarchis and has wonderful carved marble over the doors which include the Archangels Michael and Gabriel flanked by St. George and St. Theodore on the south side. The Archangel Michael has a sword in his right hand and a gruesome face on his breastplate - like the carving I referred to at Tseria. Above them is the hand of God and the dove which represents the Holy Spirit.

Next to the church, on the south side, is a restored tower house which is now a hotel called "Tsimova". To the left of the hotel entrance is a cannon, set in cement, and next to it the casing of a large World War II German bomb. To the right of the door is a barred window in which, if you peer into it, you will see a jumble of militaria which includes helmets, guns and a large machine gun of some make which I could not identify. If you enter the front door, you will meet a wonderful character called Giorgos Versakos, who will take great delight in showing you the rest of his weapons collection in a glass-fronted cabinet. It is crammed with swords, knives, guns, pistols, muskets etc - some very old and some more modern. These include, partially hidden behind everything else, an old Lewis Gun complete with drum magazine and a musket which belonged to one of Petrobey's brothers.

To see another wonderful church, drive from the northwest corner of the square (opposite the left shoulder of Petrobey's statue), and down the lane until you reach the small, vaulted church of Agios Ioannis with buttresses supporting the outside walls. Inside you will find some frescos which form a 'pictograph' of the life and death of Christ laid out in sections almost like a child's comic and this style of fresco was used as a 'visual aid' to educate the illiterate about the stories from the Bible. Parts are obscure and some liberal concrete restoration has obliterated others but you can identify incidents like the healing of a lame man holding up his bed, "Take up thy bed and walk"; the healing of a blind man; Pontius Pilate questioning Christ, who is bound and held by soldiers, followed by Pilate washing his hands and then by the mocking and scourging of Christ. You can also reach this church by walking down the narrow lane opposite the "Tsimova" tower hotel.

Continuing west from here, you drive out of the old town on a road which bears to the left towards Krilianika. You will see a small, barrel vaulted church to the right, on a small spur. Park in the lane on your right and walk to the church. It is empty and badly marked with graffiti (something I've seen nowhere else I'm pleased to say) but immediately behind it, to the east, is what appears at first sight to be a field of jumbled stone piles. If you look more closely, you will see that they are old tombs or graves - most of which are empty now. They were shallow excavations which were then "roofed" with large stones used as "rafters" which supported more rocks to cover them. Each had a small doorway, supported by a stone lintel and some still have a large rock blocking the entrance. I think they are the prototype for the modern, marble-covered graves or tombs you see in most churchyards but were never replaced by the more modern system because the church itself fell into disuse - hence the graffiti. I believe they are historically important but please respect where you are if you go to see them.

NOTE FOR WALKERS. If you are planning to walk round Mesa Mani from Areopolis, you will find accommodation at Stavri, Gerolimenas, Vathia, Porto Kayio, Marmari, Kokkala, and Kotronas so you plan your route accordingly.

# MESA MANI

## "LAND OF EVIL COUNSEL"

Mesa or Inner Mani was also known as Kakavoulia - The Land of Evil Counsel - a direct reference to the dangerous and war-like nature of the inhabitants or sometimes as Kakovounia - The Bad Mountains - which name speaks for itself. There is an alternative explanation of Kakavoulia which is that the name comes from the word for small, metal pots or cauldrons - "kakavia" - that the inhabitants frequently wore on their heads as make-shift helmets during attacks and feuds. Patrick Leigh Fermor gives much credence to this explanation in his book, "Mani" but Colonel Leake preferred the first definition - "the Land of Evil Counsel; so notorious are its inhabitants for plundering the unfortunate sailors who are cast on their tempestuous, rocky and unsheltered coast as well as for more active enterprises of robbery and piracy." His opinion is perhaps supported by a remark made to his servant by his escort. "One of the first things Tubaki said to my servant was - If the Bey had not given such precise orders concerning you, how nicely we should have stripped you of all your baggage."

There is a marked contrast with Exo Mani in that the area is much less fertile, especially on the east coast where the mountains plunge to the sea and the villages and towers perch high on the rocks in defiance of man and nature. The western side, Niklianiko, has a wide coastal plain and wherever you look you will see villages and hamlets with houses clustered for protection around the towers. Thanks to modern methods, water is more readily available now but was a common cause for feuding in former times. The conservation of water was a priority and a measure of prestige and wealth. A French traveller in the 18th Century recorded, "When a Kakavoulian gets married, his first job is to measure how much water is in the cistern because it is one of the most important dowry gifts. Whoever lavishes a lot of water on the wedding is considered rich. This extravagance makes an impression and all the region learns about how much water the in-laws drank."

The volume of refugees in the area put additional stress on the meagre resources and so water and land became the main basis for disputes and feuds because possession meant power and control. The unique architecture of the area, the towers, evolved as the means to protect these valuable assets and of course, as a defence against invaders - especially the Turks. The towers were continually manned by sentries and sometimes small garrisons to guard against attack. In 1839, the Earl of Carnavon recorded that a sentry in a tower was unable to give him directions because he had spent his entire life locked up in the tower and did not know the roads and villages of the region! A report in 1833 to the Ministry of Internal Affaires states, ".....they (the towers) are protected by them uninterruptedly. People assigned to their protection are condemned to be locked up in them and not go out for months at a time." Col. Leake recorded a tower owned by a nephew of the 5th Bey of the Mani as being permanently guarded by a garrison of 15 men in very basic conditions - "the floor consists of loose boards, and, never undergoing ablution, harbours myriads of fleas in winter and bugs in summer".

The houses protected by the towers were often rudimentary as well, with very few comforts. One explanation of this was given in 1797 by the son of Zanetbey Grigorakis who, when asked about the houses, explained "Not to whet the appetite of the Turks. Being exposed to their attacks nearly everyday, when we abandon our houses we have almost nothing to lose."

Today many of the villages are deserted except for a few elderly people and the houses and towers are collapsing and crumbling which makes the area seem even more austere and barren. A young lady who toured this area remarked to me that Mesa Mani was far too bleak and "too loaded with testosterone" for her liking. I think I know what she meant although I have to disagree. Superficially that may be the impression gained on a quick tour around the area but closer examination reveals a history as ancient as Greece herself and a wealth of artistry in the Byzantine Churches with their frescos and carved marble. Equally impressive is the construction of houses and towers in places where today, aided by modern transport and machinery, it would still be very difficult to build. Many of the houses and towers also display the pride and skill of the builders with beautiful arched marble windows and elaborate carvings on lintels and sills.

# THE MESA MANI CIRCUIT

There is a 'ring-road' that takes you down one side of Mesa Mani and back up the other and I have called this route the Mani Circuit. This is the route to take if you just want to gain an impression of the area - more detailed exploration is covered further on in the book. On the west side you drive through the wide coastal plain of the Niklianiko until you reach Alika in the South. Here you turn left and climb up into the mountains overlooking Vathia and then up the east coast to Kotronas. The scenery is spectacular and the isolated tower houses and small villages on the east coast make you marvel at the tenacity of the people who managed to build them in such steep and inaccessible places. From Kotronas you travel back to Areopolis via a high mountain pass.

## PYRGOS DIROU

Pyrgos Dirou is 10 kilometers south on the main road from Areopolis. The modern village is spread out along the main road and you turn right in the middle of the village to get to the famous Diros Caves. This junction is well signposted but you may not have time to explore the caves if you are planning to do the circuit.

The small market square on the right before this turn has a statue of "The Amazon of Pyrgos" commemorating the women who repulsed a large force of Turkish troops using only knives, rocks and sickles. The battle took place in June 1826 against the forces of Ibrahim Pasha. The Maniat men had left to defend the wall at Verga (outside Kalamata) where the Pasha's main army, having swept across the Peloponnese after the fall of Mesalongi, was attacking the Maniat defences. A force of 1,500 men was landed in the bay at Pyrgos Dirou with the objective of seizing Tsimova (Areopolis), trapping the main Maniat forces to the north and opening the road to Gythio. Ibrahim Pasha was an extremely able general and this would have been a brilliant tactic to outflank and entrap the Maniat force but he underestimated the Maniat women. When the alarm was raised, they were harvesting their crops and attacked the force in fierce 'hand to hand' combat. They were armed only with their sickles, sticks and stones but forced the Ottomans into a defensive position until reinforcements of men and more women arrived to drive them out. Only one third of the landing force escaped to their ships and the rest were destroyed. So if you meet any women carrying sickles, which are still widely used today for gathering "Horta" or wild greens - be very polite!!

The road to the caves takes you past the old village. You will see a sign advertising Mani Honey on the left side of the road and just past this, a minor road forks to the left. This takes you into part of the old village and you drive past houses and towers until you reach a large church. Take the road to the left of the church until you reach an impressive tower surrounded by a high wall. This was the tower of the Sklavounakos clan which was built on an outcrop of marble and is an impressive example of a fortified stronghold. Just past it is a small church of no particular features but it too is sitting on a marble base and next to it is a large exposed cistern cut into this bedrock. I cannot find any history of this tower but it is a magnificent fortification.

Sklavounakis Tower

The road to the caves takes you down to the bay where the Turkish force had landed and the entrance to the cave complex which includes a museum and café facilities. The museum exhibits the archaeological finds from the 'dry' cave - Alepotrypa - which prove the area was inhabited since Neolithic times, 4,500 years ago. The main attraction is the cave of Glyfada. A flight of steps takes you down to a jetty where you board a small 'punt' and travel round the flooded chambers of the cave system. Subtle lighting exhibits the wonderful colours and shapes of the stalagmites and stalactites and the overall effect is awesome.

## THE TIGANI PENINSULA AND MEZAPOS

Continuing south on the circuit, past villages and hamlets, you will see on your right the ancient 'frying pan' peninsula fortified by Guillaume de Villehardouin and subsequently occupied by a Byzantine garrison. It is believed by some historians that this is the site of the Castle of Maina but this name has also been given to a castle at Porto Kayio, so it has never been established beyond doubt but it remains the most likely candidate. It has also been suggested that the name 'Mani' originates from this castle but this too has never been proved. Very little of the castle remains and it is difficult to get to by land but it is an important Byzantine site because it also holds the ruins of a 9th Century Basilica.

The peninsula shelters the small harbour of Mezapos, once famous as a haven for pirates, and the remains of the tower of the Sassaris clan still stands near the shore. Petrobey Mavromichalis once sent a ship against the clan for resisting his attempts to gain control of the harbour and build his own tower to defend it. The Sassaris tower was damaged by cannon fire but they in turn sank the ship with their own cannon and the Mavromichalis family abandoned their ambitions in Mezapos.

The little harbour is probably the site of ancient Messa which sent ships with Agamemnon to the seige of Troy and which Pausanias called a city, but there are no signs of the ancient site.

## AGIOS YEORGIOS

To reach Mezapos, you pass through the hamlet of Agios Yeorgios, just off the main road some 14 kilometers south of Pyrgos Dirou. This is a perfect example of a small group of defensively built houses surrounding a tall war tower for additional protection and it is worth spending a short time walking round the village. There is a ruined megalithic church on your left as you leave the village towards Mezapos.

## KITA

Three kilometers further south on the main road, you come to Kita, once the most powerful village in the Niklianiko and the site of the last great inter-family feud in 1870 which was eventually suppressed by a battalion of 400 regular soldiers with artillery support. The Earl of Carnarvon recorded a feud which had raged in the town prior to his arrival. "For thirty years previously to 1839, the best blood of Kita had been drained in a deadly and embittered strife which arose out of an imaginary insult to a young girl whose scarf was held too long by her partner in the dance of some village festival. For thirty years the two factions exterminated each other; murder was not disguised, it was the avowed profession of every clansman and the recognised mode of warfare."

The towers and fortified houses of Kita are fascinating so take time to have a wander round. Many of the windows and walls of the buildings have relief carvings on them so keep a watch for these as you make your way round. A narrow road leads from behind Kita to the village of Kaloni, higher up the mountain slope, where there are more towers and fortified houses.

Lazarogonas War Tower - Kita

## NOMIA

Just below Kita, on the opposite side of the road, is Nomia - traditionally a rival village to Kita - and this too is a fascinating village to walk round. Normally, tower houses were built with the house and tower as separate components alongside each other but in Nomia there is a good example of a tower house built as a single unit by the powerful Messisklis family. The tower is five stories high and dominates the eastern side of the village, although the crack in the stonework suggests that it might not do so for much longer!. The family could man the tower from within the house while a second entrance allowed clan members access from outside. The house was originally two stories high with a marble roof.

In the yard of a small derelict house nearby is a rusty, six-foot cannon cemented into the floor. I suppose it was too heavy to shift out of the way!

## GEROLIMENAS

Traveling due south from Kita and Nomia for about 4 kilometers, you reach Gerolimenas. This fishing village and small harbour was established in about 1870 but is very much in character with the area. A tall tower stands on a cliff face overlooking the port and the small round tower close to it is in fact an old windmill. There are some old houses and small towers in Gerolimenas and it is a good place to stop for a drink or a bite to eat and there is always fresh fish on the menu at the tavernas. There is usually accommodation available here if you plan to explore the area in more detail.

Mesisklis Tower House - Nomia

## GIALI

From Gerolimenas you drive east towards Alika on the flat coastal road which is rather unattractive because of the hideous concrete houses, totally out of character, which have been built here. On your right you will see the ruins of a couple of windmills and a tower which used to protect the small anchorage of Giali. This was the harbour controlled by the Mantouvali clan of Boulari (see Further Exploration) before the development of Gerolimenas as a major port. The clan offended the Mavromichalis clan by boarding one of their ships and removing part of the cargo as "harbour dues" and they retaliated with an attack on the Mantouvali tower at Boulari. The dispute ended when one of the Mavromichalis men fell for the charms of one of the Mantavouli women who had been ferrying powder and shot to her brothers defending the tower. A truce was called, a marriage arranged and a dispute settled by a wedding feast of legendary duration and magnificence.

The anchorage looks very insignificant from the main road but if you walk to the large tower by the waters edge, you will see that it is quite large and well sheltered and that the tower affords good protection to any ship moored here. It is for the protection of shipping from pirates and Turks that the "harbour dues" were charged.

## ALIKA

Alika is some 3 kilometers from Gerolimenas and this is where you fork left to stay on the circuit but, before you do, have a wander round the village because it contains several examples of older 'megalithic' houses, characterised by their massive stone foundations and walls. There is also a good example of an older War Tower, the Philipakos Tower, as well as several more recent tower houses and tower dwellings - so a closer look at the town will give you a good idea of how these buildings developed. A small dry-stone church on your right as you leave Alika contained several snakes when I looked inside, and nothing else of particular interest, so be warned if you do venture inside! I don't think they were dangerous but it is always a bit of a shock when you stumble on a snake without warning - and when there are several......!

## MOUNTANISTIKA AND LIONTAKI

From Alika, the road climbs rapidly up the mountains towards Tsikalia and you can see a small village perched high in the mountains, in a saddle between two peaks, with the towers silhouetted against the sky. This is Mountanistika and a concrete road runs to the village from just below Tsikalia. However, it is a very narrow road with steep drops on one side and which requires great confidence to drive. It is one of the highest villages in the Mani and is virtually deserted in winter. It runs in a line along the ridge and most of the houses and towers were

Philipakos War Tower - Alika

built between 1880 and 1910. It seems extraordinary to me that towers and houses were still being built in remote areas in the same defensive styles at such a late date and more mysterious still that most of them are abandoned and derelict.

North of the ridge and slightly below Mountanistika is the tiny village of Liontaki which is linked to Mountanistika by a narrow road. I have not confirmed the name of this village because there was nobody there to ask but it is so named on an old map. The village lies in the lee of a small peak which is dominated by the two adjacent towers which can be seen perched high in the mountains above Boulari. The architecture of the buildings, which include a ruined megalithic tower, suggests that this is a much older village than Mountanistika.

From here it is possible to look out across Niklianiko to the plateau of Cavo Grosso and with good binoculars, you can make out the jumbled stones of the ruins on top of this escarpment. (see Further Exploration - Kipoula). Immediately below you is Boulari and a small gorge runs east from here, passing below Liontaki to the north and into a "hidden" valley at the top of which you can see a small hamlet. Using binoculars again, you can make out a rather strange looking church and what appears to be the ruins of a small 'castle' with two towers - one round and one square - just outside the village. You return to 'the circuit' down the same steep road and turn left at the main road to get to Tsikalia.

## TSIKALIA

Tsikalia is about 5 kilometers from Alika. The towers and houses of the village run in a line on the crest of a mountain spur which then drops dramatically to the coast far below and you have a wonderful, panoramic view of this rugged coastline. On the bend of this spur which is dominated by a restored church, on your left, you will see a small cannon mounted by the side of the road. Above the main door and below the campanile on the far side of this church, there is a curious piece of marble embedded in the wall. It appears to be part of an ancient marble carving and depicts a bull's head, yoked with a garland of fruit and flowers to another bull's head, most of which is missing. Above the garland is what appears to be a pair of "flip-flop" style sandals. I have yet to find more information on this marble and where it came from. One possible source is ancient Kainipolis on the coast below Tsikalia. (see Further Exploration - Kiparissos). A short distance beyond Tsikalia as you continue your journey eastwards, you look down on the legendary village of Vathia with its many towers crowded on the peak of a hill.

## KOROGONIANIKA AND KAINOURIA

The road now takes you across to the Eastern side of the mountains and you start to travel north again. On your right you will see a road-side shrine and a gravel road leading off to your right. If you follow this you will see a village on your left which is Korogonianika and then the road climbs higher until you reach another village which is Kainouria, I think, but there were no signs and nobody about to confirm any names. Nearby is a tangle of radio masts. I didn't see anything of particular interest in the village other than a round tower which I think was a windmill but the view from here is extraordinary. Down below you you can see the bay and harbour of Porto Kayio and and also Marmari, separated by the narrow neck of land which is dominated by the tower of Charakes. Beyond this, the tail of the Mani Peninsula runs south to Cape Matapan or Cape Tainaron - the second most southern tip of mainland Europe. You cannot see the lighthouse perched on the very end of the peninsula but it is a fantastic view and beyond it you will see the distant outline of the island of Kithira and the many ships that continually ply their trade past this landmark.

You also get a remarkable view from Korogonianika where you will also see a crumbling stone building on a small, rocky hill to the south of the village. This is an old church, constructed of large rocks, which now seems to provide a shelter for goats. There are a few frescos on the walls but they are badly faded and hard to discern. There are a number of old graves surrounding the outside of the church and some of these are collapsing so, unless you want to join the occupants, watch where you walk! Travel back by the same route to rejoin the circuit.

## LAGIA

Lagia is 5 or 6 kilometers from Tsikalia and is a typical tower village where four families lived in independently sited settlements, each with its own church. Many of the towers here were built in the older style of sloping, tapering walls while elsewhere, towers were being built with vertical walls and could consequently be built much higher. Some reached up to 20 metres with 7 floors. One of the towers in Lagia (it is claimed locally) was built overnight by 400 men of one clan to gain an advantage by sunrise!

Lagia was the home of the Mani's famous doctor, Papadakis, who kept records of all the casualties of war and feuds that he treated in the middle 18th Century. He travelled throughout the region and his records include many priests that he treated for bullet, knife, sword and rock wounds. He drew crude illustrations in the margin of his records showing the people he treated and the location and type of wound that he treated them for. Altogether he lists 700 wounded patients from 42 villages during the 53 years from 1715 to 1768. In some disputes there were more than 50 wounded in each village!

At each end of the village, just on the edge of the road on your left, are two small churches with 'tikles' roofs. The frescos in both these churches are worth stopping to see but if you have the time, you should explore the whole village because I find it even more fascinating than the famous villages of Vathia or Kita.

War Towers - Lagia

## DIMARISTIKA

Shortly after Lagia, across a small gorge around which the road follows the contours, you will see a village perched among the rocks, scrub-bushes and cacti. A sturdy tower and integrated houses dominate the craggy hilltop with defensive houses scattered below. The great swathes of cacti must surely have been encouraged to grow as a defensive measure as well as supplying "prickly pears" to supplement a meager diet. (I've heard them called "Turkish Figs" but I cannot remember where - maybe I read it in a book). The road dissects the scattered hamlet but if you imagine it being built before the road existed, you will see why I am constantly amazed by the building which took place in steep, remote areas.

## KOKKALA

Kokkala is 9 kilometers from Lagia and has small harbour and cafes and a burst of greenery compared to the barren, baked rock and prickly pear cactus that characterise the 'sunny' side of Mesa Mani. There is a small beach and many new houses and tavernas here and it no longer has the characteristics of a typical Mani village but you are sure of a friendly welcome if you stop for a drink or a bite to eat. It probably developed after the War of Independence because its location would have made it very vulnerable to attack from the sea.

## NYFI

Nyfi (Nymfi on some maps) is about 7 kilometers beyond Kokkala and was yet another village with six different clan/family strongholds in their own areas and which dominated this part of Sunny Mani. There was inter-clan warfare reported here as late as 1862 between the Bourikos and Ventikos families. The buildings higher up are older than the comparatively newer houses closer to the road and there is a wonderful collection of towers of various shapes and sizes, including the relatively new Ventikos Tower which stands out from the rest for its imposing height and unusual number of windows. There are roads leading up to these towers from both ends of the village but you cannot drive through the upper section so you have to return by whichever route you take. If you walk around this area you will see the many towers and several megalithic houses.

## DRYALI AND ARGILIA

Continuing north, you will see two villages perched high above the main road. The first is Dryali and the second is Argilia but to reach them you must travel further north until you see a road off to your left which doubles back towards the south and gradually climbs up to these villages. The road is not too good in some places, so be warned if you decide to drive there. At the risk of repeating myself too often, you cannot help but marvel at the people who built these villages in such inaccessible places. You will understand  exactly what I mean when you see them.

## FLOMOCHORI

Some 7 kilometers or so from Kokkala, this village is similar in that it obviously benefits from a reasonable water supply in the narrow coastal strip on which it lies. There are several impressive war towers in the village and again it is worth wandering round the village on foot to have a closer look at them. The close proximity of some of these towers suggests a history of rivalry and feuding but I cannot find any historic information on this village. Shortly after leaving the village you come to a junction. To reach Kotronas you turn right or you can go straight on to get back to Areopolis. If you go to Kotronas,  only 3 kilometers away, you will double back to this junction to get back to Areopolis.

## KOTRONAS

Kotronas is a delightful fishing port with a couple of towers, seafront tavernas and a small beach. It provides the opportunity to cool off with a refreshing dip in the sea and from here you can look back along the route you have just driven. It has been identified as the ancient town of Teuthrone which Pausanias visited and where he recorded "the god they worship most is Issorian Artemis and they have a spring called Naia." It was also one of the Free Lakonian Cities.

The main part of Teuthrone seems to have been the small island of Skopa, now linked by a causeway to the mainland. Here there is evidence of mediaeval masonry suggesting a sizeable castle but I cannot find any reference to such. There is a restored church on the island with old marble built into it. The land is private and there is little to see by way of "ruins" but it is one of the most beautiful and peaceful places I have been to and I spent some time just sitting absorbing the tranquil atmosphere.

To the east, in the mountains high above Kotronas, you will see what appears to be a walled castle. It is the Monastery of Sotira and is not easy to reach but you can get closer to it if you take the road which leads off to the right from a small square as you travel back through Kotronas from the harbour. The road turns into rough track so you will have to walk. The monastic cells and various other buildings are in ruins but the church has been restored. Just outside the monastery walls you will see two rows of stone-made, open ended 'boxes' with one row built on top of the other. These are old beehives of a type that Leake noticed on his travels in the area and which you may come across elsewhere.

## LOUKADIKA

The road climbs a steep, meandering route to this village on your way back to Areopolis. The tight cluster of houses at the top of the village used to be a castle which the locals still call the Kastro and there is evidence of an early megalithic settlement here.

## CHIMARA

The only reference I have found to this small village is that it too was an early megalithic settlement. There are some old towers and houses and, north of the village, what appears to be a collection of ruined buildings which I have not yet explored.

## PYRRICHOS or KAVALOS

Kavalos is about 10 kilometers from Kotronas and has been renamed Pyrrichos which was the ancient name for this village but, depending on which map you use, you may find either name. Pausanias suggests it was named after Pyrros - Achilles' son - or alternatively, a rather obscure god called Silenos-Pyrrichos who was a god of water sources in stony mountain villages. There was a well here said to have been given by Silenos and there were sanctuaries to 'Unwarlike Artemis' and 'Amazonian Apollo' because the Amazon expedition stopped its advance here. It too was one of the Free Lakonian Cities and a Roman settlement. There are several old tower houses and towers here in various stages of collapse and there are, I'm told, the remains of a Roman Baths but I cannot find them.

From here the road continues west through the pass for about 4 kilometers until it rejoins the main road just south of Areopolis and so completes The Mani Circuit.

## MESA MANI - FURTHER EXPLORATION

In addition to travelling round The Circuit, there are many other interesting places to explore in Mesa Mani and here follows a few suggestions of readily accessible villages and one or two places which are not quite so accessible.

### GLEZOS

Travelling south from Pyrgos Dirou, just after leaving the town, you will see a concrete road on your left with a small signpost to Glezos. Follow this road, which turns into a reasonable track, and bearing right, you will see the Church of St. Michael (Agios Stratigos) through the trees. It is an 11th Century cruciform church with stone buttresses and a few re-used bits of marble to support the walls. Inside there are only fragments of frescos left exposed and one of these appears to be the Archangel Michael after whom the church is named. There are some well carved, old tiebeams supporting the dome but the templon is much more recent. The bits of marble set in the buttresses may well have come from an old templon.

Agios Stratigis - Glezos

# CHAROUDA

Continuing south on the main road, about 2 kilometers south of Pyrgos, you will see signs for Triandafilia and Charouda on your right. Take this turning, pass through the first village and continue to Charouda. As you drive through the village you will see one or two ruined megalithic houses and, on a bend, a ruined megalithic church. Continue to the outskirts of the village and you will reach the beautiful 11th Century church of St. Michael, partially hidden behind a high wall with a gate that gives access to the courtyard. The church has a tall, marble campanile which contains several pieces of old marble but, like most of the churches, this is a more recent addition. The door of the church has a wonderful carved lintel and step and, walking round the outside of the church, you cannot fail to notice the massive rectangular blocks of marble, interspersed with sandstone blocks, with which the walls have been constructed. The intricate cloisonné brickwork decorations are also extremely fine. On the north side of the church is what appears to be the square base of a tower and on top of it is a massive bell.

At the east end of the church is the graveyard and the outside walls of the three apses contain some more decorated marble blocks. One of these has a curious carving showing a long-bodied animal with a face which is turned towards you and which has enormous 'Mickey Mouse' ears. This animal, rather like a Centaur, is firing a bow and arrow at another animal which looks similar to a deer rearing up on its hind legs. There is also an inscription which is very difficult to make out. Another ancient, rectangular marble has been set upside down in the wall and this has an inscription crudely scratched on it which is hard to decipher.

The church contains some wonderful frescos but many have been damaged by smoke and by water seepage. The whole of the narthex has been whitewashed and the keyholder explained that this was because it made the women who stood there uncomfortable to turn their backs on the Saints who adorned the rear walls! The marble tie beams and decorations on the templon are fantastic but most remarkable of all was the ring of decorated marble which runs round the base of the dome. The demand to see this church is very high and the keyholder keeps a low profile in summer or else she would spend all her time unlocking and locking the church and be unable to do anything else. The best time to catch her is in the late afternoon or early evening when she goes to the church to clean it, light candles etc.

In the field to the west of the church are several very large, ruined megalithic houses which are fascinating because it is so difficult to imagine working with such large stones without the benefit of a mechanical crane. This is especially true when you see the massive lintels that were placed over the doorways. This megalithic village can only be dated by excavation and identification of the finds that are revealed but this has not been done.

As you return to the main road, if you look carefully at the rising hills to the east, you will see the dome of another church nestled among some cypress trees. To reach it you turn south on the main road and then, after only a couple of hundred yards, turn left on a narrow concrete road. Follow this up the hill and it too turns into a track. At the 'T' junction, turn right and you will see a broken road running further up the hill on your left. You can risk the car if you like, or walk up the road until you see a track running to your left to the church. This is another 11th Century church and is dedicated to St. Peter. It is not in good condition but it has a lovely setting which makes the visit worthwhile. There is a ruined church immediately beside it and some of the marble from this appears to have been re-used for St. Peter's.

## DRYALOS, VAMVAKA, BRIKI and MINA

A short distance further south (approx 2 kilometers) on the main road, there is a road which goes off to your left to Dryalos, Vamvaka, Briki and Mina. It starts off well but is quite rough in places. Briki was a monastic community and here there are four Byzantine churches - two are in ruins, one has been 'restored' and the fourth, Agios Nikolaos, contains some fine 14th Century frescos. Vamvaka has the church of Agios Theodoros dated 1075 with some wonderful carved marble as does the church in the middle of Dryalos, especially on the bell tower.

The Church of Agios Theodoros is in a sad state which is a terrible shame. Above the door there are intricately carved marble decorations, partly eroded on one side by the rubbing of the rope which was used to ring the church bell above the doorway. There are more carvings around the door and on the tie beams and templon inside the church. There is a very striking fresco of the Virgin Mary behind the templon but this is the only fresco which has survived. Unless action is taken soon, this church is bound to succumb to old age and another beautiful Byzantine church will fall into ruins. Already there is what amounts to a small tree growing out of the south wall, about 8 feet from the ground, and I shudder to think what the roots of this are doing to the structure of the wall.

You can also reach these villages along tarmac roads which run from the main road. Look out for the signposts directing you and this may be a better option rather than risk a puncture or damage to your car.

## TSOPAKAS AND TRISSAKIA

Continuing south for about another 2 kilometers, look out for a small sign on your right which points to Tsopakas and St. Barbara. Turn here and follow the road into the village. You will see a low wall on your right and if you stop and look over this, there is a massive 'crater' on the other side. It appears to be a collapsed cave and must be about 25 to 30 metres deep. The floor is covered in shrubs and trees but it is an astonishing sight. Half way down the south face of the hole, you can see the remains of some sort of stone fortification with a cave behind it.

If you carry on through the village the road turns into track but, if you go carefully (or walk), this takes you out among the olive trees and you come to a water-filled, open cistern on the far side of which is the derelict church of Trissakia. It is actually three barrel-vaulted churches side by side with a main church in the middle which is flanked by two smaller chapels. It looks a mess, which indeed it is, but if you enter the main church by the very low west door, and keep an eye on the gaping hole in the roof as you do so - in case of falling stones - you will see why I have included it in this guide. At the east end is a wonderful, carved marble templon which, given the very ordinary exterior of the church, is totally unexpected. It is still intact and close examination shows that the marble has been worked by exceptional craftsmen but I doubt it will remain undamaged for much longer as there is another hole in the roof above the sanctuary which will surely erode more and more until the whole place collapses.

The main body of the church was once covered in frescos but the only really discernable ones remaining are of the Last Supper and the seizing of Christ in the Garden of Gethsemane. These too are doomed to destruction as the church crumbles. It is easy to identify Judas at the Last Supper because he has been painted smaller than the the rest and without a halo and looks to me like a naughty boy, while the disciples appear to regard him with contempt or disdain. The large crack running through this fresco heralds its ultimate fate.

## ERIMOS

Travelling on the main road south from here, just after a turn to your right to Lakkos, you will see another sign showing Erimos off to your right. Follow this road down through the olives and you pass a ruined megalithic building on the road side. It is an old derelict church with a single marble column still visible inside among the jumble of stones. Continuing along the road you reach Erimos and on the other side of the village you will see the 12th Century church of St. Barbara. When I last went there it was being restored, with scaffolding around the Cupola and building materials scattered about, but still worth seeing for the elaborate cloisonné brickwork decoration and the carved marble, especially on the panels set in the windows. In an adjacent field is a derelict church with most of the outer stone blocks removed. Whoever built it hid an earthenware 'bottle' in the wall but whatever it contained has been found because a hole has been made in its side and it is now empty.

## GARDENITSA

Another church worth seeing is just a little further south on the main road at Kato Gardenitsa. Ignore the sign for Pano Gardenitsa and continue a little further and turn right at the sign for Kato Gardenitsa, less than a kilometer before you come to Kita. A concrete road takes you into the village where you will see the 11th Century church of Agios Sotiras (St Saviour) on your right, with a ruined tower nearby. It has a domed outer narthex or entrance porch supported on arches which are in turn supported by marble pillars and the effect is very pleasing although it is probably a later addition. The doorway has some rather crude carved marble crosses and designs and unfortunately I got no further because it was locked and there was nobody about to ask for a keyholder and, being a holiday, I didn't like to knock on any doors. Even more frustrating, I could smell incense burning inside and a look through the window showed lit candles so I had just missed finding it open.

In "Deep into Mani", Peter Greenhalgh says that this church and Agios Stratigos at Boulari are the only two churches with a domed porch in the Mani. I suspect that the Church of Agios Petros in Kastania also had a similar feature - now disguised by a "tikles" roof. (see page 44).

Agios Sotiras - Gardenitsa

## TOURLOTI

Returning to the main road from Gardenitsa, turn left and drive north again for about 100 metres and then turn right along an unsurfaced road for a short distance until you reach a truly beautiful small church on your right. The church is 12th century and has beautiful cloisonné brick patterns on the upper half around the windows and a very attractive pattern of large stone blocks make up the lower half. It was locked but standing on a large boulder at the rear of the church, I could see through the window. The capitals of the columns that support the dome are carved marble as are the beams but I could see no frescos. Next to the church, a pile of stones shows the outline of another church which has been reduced to rubble. I had the great good fortune to meet a family from Athens here and the grandfather studied Byzantine Churches as a hobby. He translated the inscription above the door as a dedication to the Saints Sergius and Bacchus and to St. George, written in what he called "Byzantine Greek" but he could not read the date except to say it was eleven hundred and something. He said this was his favourite Mani church and, as if to prove it, kept stroking and patting the walls like a family pet . His two young grandsons kept asking him questions and it was obvious that they too were inspired by his enthusiasm - a wonderful gift to pass on to another generation.

Agios Sergios & Vachos - Tourloti

# MINI CIRCUIT

Further south, before you reach Kita, there is a road off to your right signposted Stavri. This road takes you on a circuit below the escarpment of Cavo Grosso and returns you to the main road below Kita. You pass through many towered villages and settlements and you will see innumerable churches lying among the olive groves. There are also many small roads leading off this circuit to villages like Keria, Ochia and Kipoula. (See below)

## STAVRI

This is a typical Mani village but also presents one of the few opportunities for good accommodation in the area. The 'Tsitsiris Castle' Hotel offers rooms in very well restored towers which, combined with the atmosphere of the setting, makes it a wonderful base for exploring this area.

## KIPOULA AND CAVO GROSSO

Between Stavri and Kounos on the Mini Circuit, there is a turnoff to the right which takes you to the village of Kipoula and behind it or above it on the ridge of Cavo Grosso is possibly the site of ancient Hippola which was deserted in Pausanias's time but where he records there was a sanctuary of Athene. Archaeologists debate the exact site but on the ridge there is ample evidence of early occupation and there have been finds of coins and pottery below the ridge so maybe, as one theory goes, Hippola was at both these sites.

It is not easy to climb the ridge but there are paths winding their way up to the defensive wall which lines the cliff edge. If you turn North at the top and walk along the western edge of the plateau, you will pass six derelict churches and a positive maze of old stone walls. The last two churches are not completely derelict and one of them contains fluted marble columns and other carved marbles which have obviously come from an earlier temple or building. A deep cistern between the two churches has frogs living in it. I cannot begin to imagine how they got here, and they cannot get out, so presumably they will evolve into a unique species - if they are not unique already!

Among the ruins here, there are good examples of megalithic houses - a couple of which also had towers. The view from the escarpment gives you a better idea of how many villages there are in Niklianiko, although you cannot see them all because some are hidden in dead ground. You also have a good view of Tigani below you to the north and on a clear day, you can see as far as Areopolis!

The ruins to the south of the plateau are amazing. At the narrowest point, between the sea cliffs and the cliffs above Kipoula, there is a defensive wall which is 10 to 12 feet thick with one tiny doorway on its entire length. There are a few scattered buildings to the south of it but the wall effectively protects a mass of derelict buildings and stone walls which must have been a substantial settlement.

South of this wall, the plateau rises to a low hill with a 'Trig' point on the summit. To the east of it, on the edge of the escarpment, is the ruins of another barrel-vaulted church with a few fresco fragments remaining. Beyond this is another hill with the village of Dri below the escarpment. There is a ruined church on the summit of this hill with some old marble but I searched in vain for a statue base with the feet still attached. It was recorded as being here so I can only hope that it was removed by some authority rather than a "treasure hunter".

South of this hill is a fairly steep track which takes you down to the village of Dri but you can walk past here to the end of the plateau before you make the descent. Assuming you have left a car at Kipoula, you then have a pleasant walk back through the olive groves and pastures below the escarpment to your start point. The terrain on the escarpment is rough and thorny and almost impassable in some places, so wear stout boots and trousers if you go up there and take water with you.

In the village of Kipoula is a remarkable "church within a church". The outer church is a large, unfinished building without a roof and inside is a small, barrel-vaulted church. The outer church was built about a hundred years ago but the man who was financing it died and it was never completed. The inner church is older and was going to be dismantled once the outer was completed. The interior of the small church has been painted over and only fragments of frescos remain but there are some interesting bits of marble embedded in the outer walls including an ancient gravestone lying on its side. This is just to the right if you enter the outer church through the south door and you can make out two figures - one appears to be carrying a vase or jug and the other larger figure has sadly lost its head. There is a similar tombstone embedded in the church at Keria.

## KOUNOS and KERIA

If you rejoin the mini circuit and travel south, you will come to the village of Kounos - a typical Niklian village with many towers in various conditions. To return to the main road just keep going but if you turn right along a narrow concrete road which you will see in the village, this takes you further south until you come to a T-junction. You turn right here to reach the village of Dri but if you look to your left you will see a small hamlet which consists of a few houses and buildings on either side of the road. This is Keria and here you will find a wonderful church.

The church is dedicated to St. John (Agios Ioannis) and was built in the 13th Century using a great variety of carved marble set in the outer walls, including part of an ancient tombstone which is laid horizontaly to the right of the door and shows two women and two men holding hands as though saying a fond farewell. A small marble panel depicts a man dressed in a toga with a small dog at his feet and it looks to me as though he is showing or offering it a dead rabbit or hare.

The dog appears to be sniffing at the object. Another panel shows a mounted soldier wearing a plumed helmet and 'fustanella' or 'kilt'. He is armed with a spear and round shield and there is a snake on the ground with a large bird stood nearby. Much of the marble has obviously been 'quarried' from older buildings and while some, like the tombstone, are ancient, some of the others are intricately patterned and obviously more recent and presumably come from an earlier church in the area. These include some large, intricately carved blocks which look as though they may have been the panels of an iconostasis or templon. I still haven't found the keyholder for this church which is said to contain more marbles and frescos but the trip is still worthwhile just to examine the exterior.

Agios Ioannis - Keria

## OCHIA

When you leave Keria, turn right and drive down the hill. Off to your right you will see the village of Ochia with 12th Century church of Agios Nikolaos set just outside the village and recognisable by a large, 3 tier belltower. Take the first right turn to reach the village which has a few towers and a curious double church with two separate entrances and a tiny door connecting the two inside. To find these, you turn right by an old tower with a gaping hole in the base in the center of the village and just beyond it, on your right, you will find the churches. They are dedicated to Agios Petros (St. Peter) and Panagia (Virgin Mary) and there are the remains of some frescos inside and in one, the doorway of the templon is made of two large pillars with a large lintel perched precariously above them.

The road that leads to the church of Agios Nikolaos passes a large old, megalithic building which does not appear to have any entrance. It may cover an old cistern but I've no firm idea of what it is or was. The church of Agios Nikolaos has a restored cupola with a concrete covered dome which, being devoid of tiles, gives it the appearance of being bald. The very solid, square campanile has many relief decorations on it but the pyramid roof has lost its tip.

If you are interested in Ornithology, this area was 'swarming' with Hoopoe and Shrike and a host of other small birds in early spring. I saw at least six Hoopoe at Ochia alone and the entire area was literally carpeted with the most amazing display of wild flowers but these disappear as the land becomes parched and desiccated by the summer sun.

Hoopoe

## KATO and ANO BOULARI

Driving south from Kita for about 5 kilometers, shortly before you reach Gerolimenas, there is a turning on your left to Boulari. There are effectively two villages, Kato & Ano or Upper and Lower Boulari. The tower defended by the Mantouvalos clan against the Mavromichalis clan (see Mani Circuit - Giali) dominates the main street of the upper village and a little further on is the much older Anemodouras Tower which may be as early as the 17th Century when the village was recorded as having a population of 40 families. This was built with huge stones without mortar and rises from walls two metres thick at the base to 80 cms thick at the top. Access to the tower was from the house which 'leans' on one of the outer walls and both the house and tower originally had marble roof tiles. A second house has been added to the first at a later date.

Further up the village, past the modern church, you come to a derelict church with only the former sanctuary remaining intact. This now has a door and is preserved like a small chapel. If you walk on up the hill from here in the direction of two towers high up on a hill (see Mani Circuit - Liontaki), you will come to the beautiful 11th Century church of Agios Stratigos. It is famous for the frescos inside but again I cannot find a keyholder and the church is always locked. The grave yard has some old graves covered with "tikles". It used to be customary to use the tikles from church roofs to cover graves and this accounts for the damage and destruction of many frescos which then suffered from rain seeping through the damaged roofs. The church gives the impression of sinking into the landscape and this is accentuated by the colour of the stone blocks and tikles tiles which are the same as the surrounding, rocky hillsides. The cupola is crude compared to the elaborate cupolas of later churches and it too, like Agios Nikolaos at Ochia, has lost its tiles except for a 'fringe' around the base. It also has a small dome over the enclosed narthex, like the church at Gardenitsa, and I have read that these are the only two churches in the Mani with that particular feature although I suspect that the Church of St. Peter at Kastania in Exo Mani may have had a similar feature at one time.

In another section of Ano Boulari stands the war tower of Theodorakakis within its own complex. It was built after the War of Independence and has a good example of a 'diavatico' or vaulted passageway as a defensive feature to make access more difficult.

There are other towers in the two villages and a large number of churches of various ages and designs and in varying conditions of disrepair. Most of these churches were locked when I tried to see inside them - except for the 'derelict' ones - but it is still interesting to wander the streets and narrow alleyways of these villages and catch a glimpse of a bygone era.


## VATHIA TO PORTO KAYIO

To reach this area you travel east from Gerolimenas until you reach Alika and here you turn right at the T-junction which is signposted to Vathia and Porto Kayio. The road from Alika drops down a hill to a small village with a few towers and houses on either side of the main road. There is no signpost but this is the village of Kiparissos.

## KIPARISSOS

This is the city that Pausanias called "Kainipolis whose name was formerly Tainaron", a member of the Union of Free Lakonians and the most important port south of Mezapos. It appears to have risen to prominence during the Roman Period and it was here in 468 AD that Genseric's Vandals tried to land from North Africa in an attempt to conquer the Peloponnese. They were defeated and gave up the attempt. Pausanias recorded a sanctuary of Demeter and a shrine of Aphrodite "on the seashore with a standing stone statue".

There is still ample evidence of Classic times. A little church which stands on a small headland east of the harbour has marble used in its construction which includes column capitols, a block of marble with a Latin inscription and other pieces, one of which may be part of the lid of a sarcophagus. Inside the church, a marble slab which serves as the altar is inscribed to the "City of Tainarion".

To appreciate the site of the city, climb the hill on the headland to the ruined tower. Looking down you can see massive dry stone walls where the ruins of the town have been cleared for olive trees but they give the outline of a substantial settlement. Some of these walls are over twelve feet high and most are several feet thick. The tower may well occupy the site of a temple judging by the marble foundations still embedded there and on the headland to the east I found parts of marble columns in a jumbled heap. This might have been a small church, judging by the outline of the stones on which these columns are lying, or they may mark the site of a former temple.

Looking down from the tower towards the modern village you can make out the ruins of the church of St. Peter where more marble columns are scattered around and two inscribed stelae were used to make the west door. This church is dated to the early 6th century and cited by some as evidence of the early Christian conversion of the Mani.

Behind the tower, about 50 metres towards the sea and concealed by some very vicious thorn scrub are the foundations of another possible temple site. Large marble blocks outline a rectangular building but I could not find the inscribed marble stelae which I had read were also at this site.

Below this, on the south east edge of the headland overlooking the tiny harbour is another church where several old columns have been used to construct the boundary wall of a forecourt and there is also a modern bust of a typical Maniat warrior with his splendid moustaches.

The wall of the church is covered with carved marble and stone symbols, some of which are recent, and there are old column capitals inside the church. The church does not face to the east which suggests it may be built on much older foundations. Immediately behind this church, there are some more old pieces of marble of various shapes and sizes built into the walls and the outline of the foundations of what may have been an old church but they are so overgrown that I cannot be sure. Lying on the ground is a curious, rectangular stone on top of which is a stone cylinder with two holes in it. It would seem that the cylinder was rolled back and forth on the rectangular stone to grind corn or crush olives, but I cannot be certain. (It strongly resembles a corn mill from the Mayan civilization of ancient Mexico - so that is where I got the idea from!).

The site of the Temple of Aphrodite to which Pausanias referred is thought to be at the western side of the hill where a dry river bed runs into a sheltered bay. Here there is a ruined tower and in the area behind it, the ruins of the church of Agia Paraskevi with a statue base dedicated to the Emperor Gordian. You can see where the feet of the statue were fixed to the base but the inscription is faded in several places. There are a few marbles scattered here and some more in the ruined house towards the beach near the tower. Be careful exploring here, especially with children, because I found three uncovered wells inside the walled area. They were overgrown and hidden by shrubbery and easy to fall into.

## VATHIA

If you continue along the main road for about 4 kilometers, you come to Vathia which is the towered village that features in most of the travel brochures and other advertisements for the Mani. When first seen in the distance perched high on the summit of a hill, it reminds me of Hollywood's version of legendary Camelot! The modern road takes you up the hill into the village where some of the towers have been restored and are used for holiday accommodation. It is a fascinating cluster of tower houses and war towers where the proximity of feuding families must have made it an extremely dangerous place to live or even to visit - so much so that Colonel Leake and his party bypassed it. "At 8.30 the sea is near us on the right hand and the village (Vathia) half a mile on our left. We halt five minutes to allow time to Gika and Poliko to answer the inquiries of a party of armed men from Vathia, who meet us on the road. This village, my guides say, has been divided into two parties for the last forty years, in which time they reckon that about 100 men have been killed".

Vathia

## THE BAY OF PORTO KAYIO

Beyond Vathia, the road meanders above the rocky coastline and there are isolated houses and towers and some wonderful scenery. After about 4 kilometers you come to an unsurfaced road on your left with a signpost to Lagia. This road forks within 100 meters and a newly bulldozed road runs off to the left to Lagia and the right fork takes you round the north side of the bay of Porto Kayio to a former monastery and a castle. A large church marks the site of the monastery and beyond this the road passes a fertile gully fed by a mountain spring which emerges from the rock by the roadside. This gully used to be a dramatic splash of greenery but much of the flora was destroyed by a fire which swept the hillsides in the summer of 1997. (A stark reminder of the danger of fire during the hot, dry summers and a warning to be careful, especially with discarded cigarettes). The road follows the contour round the side of the slope until you reach the high curtain walls of the castle. There are new and restored houses here but you can still see that the castle was a formidable bastion which the Turks built in 1570 to protect the anchorage from use by pirates and as a base for naval operations against the Venetian lines of supply to Cyprus. Within a year of the Turks establishment here, the Maniats, with naval support from the Venetians, attacked and captured the fortress. When Crete was captured by the Turks in 1669, they also subdued the Mani which had supported the Venetian defence of Crete and re-occupied the castle. It changed hands again fifteen years later and was again recaptured by the Turks thirty years after that but I cannot find any details of how long they held it on this occasion but it would certainly have been retaken in the early 1780's when the Maniats sacked Passava Castle.

Returning to the main road, turn left and within a few yards there is another fork in the road. The left fork takes you to Porto Kayio and the right to Marmari which you can see on the cliff top above two small sandy beaches with the Charakes Tower dominating the high ground between both villages. Heading towards Porto Kayio you pass the summit of a hill on your right where you will see a small church and some graves. (If you plan to walk to the end of the peninsula this is a good starting point. From the church, a path leads to a larger church and the main track south). The road then winds down the hill to the secluded beach and village of Porto Kayio where you can get refreshments at one of the tavernas and accommodation if you want to stay here and break your journey.

It is almost certain that Porto Kayio is ancient Psamathus which Pausanias and other writers referred to but of which there is no trace now. There are some twenty tombs cut into the rock high on a ridge to the southwest of the port but I haven't found them yet. They date from the Hellenistic period and are thought to be those of mercenaries, many of whom congregated in this area in classical times and much later, to offer their services to passing ships.

A short walk to the mouth of the bay brings you to a monument to Lambros Katsonis. He held a commission from the Russian Imperial Court and operated against Turkish shipping under the Russian flag until 1792 when the Russians made peace with the Sultan. He had installed a gun battery on the northern slopes of the bay and assembled a small flotilla to attack Turkish shipping but could not resist supplementing his income by attacking any other ship which looked likely to return a profit. He paid dearly for an attack on two French ships at Nafplio. A French warship supported an attack on Porto Kayio by a Turkish fleet, destroyed the gun battery, captured his flotilla and Katsonis was forced to flee overland. The bay was also used as one of the escape routes for allied troops cut off by the German occupation of Greece during the 2nd World War.

To reach Marmari from here, you must retrace your steps back to the road junction and turn left.

## MARMARI

As you approach Marmari, a road leads off to your left. This is the main route down south to ancient Tainaron. Marmari is probably ancient Achilleus, a small harbour in classical times which was mentioned by Pausanias and other historians but of no great significance because they gave no details other than the name. The first building you reach is a taverna with rooms to let and a path leads from here down to the first small, sandy beach. The main part of the village sits on the cliffs where it can be more easily defended and then another path leads down the steep slopes from the village to the sandy bay where the ancient harbour used to be. An astonishing site at Marmari, and many other places in the Mani, are the old terraces on the steep hillsides high above the village. The effort needed to build these for the cultivation of wheat or corn is mindblowing and illustrates the lengths people had to go to in order to survive in this harsh environment.

## PALIROS, ASOMATI AND CAPE TAINARON

To continue your journey south, return to the junction you passed as you approached Marmari but - be warned if you are driving - that although the road starts well, it is rough and unsurfaced in places and you run a high risk of punctures. (I've driven this route twice and met cars with punctures on both occasions).

The road takes you past an astonishingly large church to a junction. The road to the left goes to Paliros and the road to the right takes you further south. Paliros is an old village with an amazing number of houses being restored or already completed. Continuing your journey south, you come to a track on your right with a signpost pointing to Mianes. It is very unsuitable for a car so if you want to go there you will have to walk. (I've never been but I'm told it is a deserted hamlet of just a few houses which are sometimes used to pen goats). The road continues south and on your left you catch glimpses of secluded inlets and small bays with shingle beaches and scattered, ruined buildings. You finally reach a few scattered houses and a taverna and below you is the Bay of Asomati and the ancient city of Tainaron. Standing on the small promontory which juts out into the sea between two small beaches is the ruined church of Asomati, from which the bay is named, and which may have been the site of the Temple of Poseidon. This has never be proved, but a temple to Poseidon stood here for over a thousand years and was known throughout the ancient world as a sanctuary. Parts of this ruined church are constructed with massive stone blocks which could be ancient masonry. Col. Leake visited this site and, examining the outside of the building, he noted, "This altar end is formed in part of Hellenic masonry, not quite regular; the stones, though very large, being not all quadrangular. At the end of this piece of Hellenic wall, near the altar, a narrow ancient door remains, which is not apparent from within, having been immured in converting the temple into a church. Several other parts of the church walls are formed of ancient wrought blocks, but that which is to the right of the altar only is original in its construction and site." He also noted that the church was not aligned to the east. His description is still valid today and the point he was making is that the church was built using part of the temple, or another ancient building which was still standing in situ and not just by using blocks which were scattered around the general area. The doorway he refers is still visible on the outside of the church but, exactly as he noted, it does not give access to the inside.

The entrance to hell or Hades was also reputed to be at this ancient site. Pausanias traveled here and recorded, "Some of the Greek poets have written that at this place Herakles brought up the hound of Hades, yet no road leads underground through the cave nor is it credible that the gods should have an underground house where they collected the souls of the dead." Apart from the apparent heresy of denying the possible existence of Hades, his disappointment with the cave is still evident today. It is situated to the north of the church on the shore of the small cove, screened by shrubs and trees and used now to store the paraphernalia of the local fishing boats. The floor is just as solid as it was two thousand years ago.

Pausanias went on to write, "Among other dedications at Tainaron is Arion the musician in bronze on a dolphin. Herodotus told the story of Arion and the dolphin from hearsay in his records of Lydia; and I have seen the dolphin at Poroselene showing its gratitude to a boy who cured it when it was wounded by fishermen; I saw it come when he called it and carry him when he wanted to ride on it. There was also a water spring at Tainaron which works no miracles these days, but once (so they say) if you looked into the water it would show you the harbours and ships. A woman stopped the water from ever showing such sights again by washing dirty clothes in it." The water spring would have been invaluable in this arid area but there is no sign of it now. There are many cisterns, however, scattered among the outlines of the foundations of what must have been a substantial town. These are clearly visible both north and south of the promontory and the church and it is possible to make out small roads, houses and steps cut into the rocks while here and there are more, large, rectangular blocks of masonry.

Among the jumble of foundations to the south, alongside a goat track which may have once been a narrow road, lie the remains of a mosaic floor. Now partially destroyed by plants growing through it, it appears to have been the floor of a small, rectangular room and consists of a white disc set in small brick tiles. The disc contains a pattern of brown tiles which form a 'stylized' wave pattern. Inside this a is a brown circle inside which is a very basic six petalled flower. Adjacent is another crude mosaic of larger, random tiles, almost totally destroyed, with the same small, brick tiles surrounding it. To me it suggests an external patio with a small entrance hall - created to give a good impression to any visitor - but then my imagination enjoys these speculations which have no archaeological foundation!

If you walk over the next ridge to the south, you will reach the lighthouse which stands on the southern tip of mainland Greece. I have never made the trip because I have always spent too long exploring the old foundations and run out of time! One day perhaps....

# PASSAVA

I have labeled the area which is south of the Areopolis to Gythio road as the Passava area. It extends from Kouskouni, just outside Areopolis, to Gythio and as far south as the Bay of Skoutari.

## KOUSKOUNI

This is the small village you can see on the mountainside to the east of Areopolis. To reach it you drive towards Gythio and take the first tarmac road on the right, just past some houses, and this doubles back to the village. There is a restored church, Metamorphosis, which was locked but the terrace outside gives you a wonderful view of Areopolis and the country to the south of the town. I found nothing else of particular interest but was surprised to see how small Areopolis really is.

## VACHOS

Traveling east on the main road you will see a sign for Skala Vachos. This track is rough in places and takes you through a small village of no particular interest before going on to Vachos along an even worse track, so don't take this route!

The best road is further east towards Gythio where there is a small crossroads and a couple of houses, 5 kilometers from Areopolis.. The road to the left leads to Kelefa Castle and to the right takes you to Vachos, 1 kilometer away.

Col. Leake said of Vachos - "Zanim Bey lives at Vakho which consists of about thirty miserable huts." He was referring to Zanetbey Grigorakis who withdrew to here from Mavrovouni when he was being actively pursued by the Turks. Today it is much improved and sits on the side of a steep hill overlooking a fertile valley. Vachos has two large churches, both of which seem to be quite new. I saw nothing else of particular interest except two circular "plaques" set in the wall of a building next to the eastern end of the large church in the square. These had been painted and I'm not sure what they represent although one seemed to be a man killing a serpent or dragon (St. George?).

## DROSOPIGIS and NEOCHORI

Driving east from Vachos, you travel through very pleasant countryside and soft rolling hills until you reach a fork in the road. Don't go left - it turns into a bad track which eventually reaches the main Areopolis to Gythio road. The road to the right takes you up to the small village of Drosopigis with a few ruined towers and fortified houses, about 4 kilometers from Vachos.

The road continues through some wonderful scenery and a great view to the east of Skoutari Bay, Skoutari and Parasiros and then reaches Neochori. As you approach Neochori, you pass a strange triple tower which looks as though "Mad

King Ludwig of Bavaria" had a hand in its construction! This village has a couple of ruined towers and a small Kafeneon. Turn left at the church and you reach a whitewashed church where the road turns left down towards Karyoupoli. If you carry straight on you reach Kavki, a small hamlet with a restored tower which is being lived in but there is little to see here.

## KARYOUPOLI (Miniakova)

Just before you reach the main road to Gythio, there is a tarmac road on your right which climbs up to Karyoupoli. First you pass a small ruined tower then turn left past the splendid Kosanakos tower into the small square with the restored church of St. Peter. (Locked when I visited).

Kosanakos Tower - Karyoupoli

Karyoupoli was the fortified complex of the Phokas-Kavalierakis family. The family moved from Kelefa after Thomas Phokas was made a Knight of St. Mark by the Venetians for his efforts on their behalf and the 'Kavalierakis' (Cavalier) part of the name commemorates this title. The tower has a substantial house attached and immediately behind it are the gates to another fortified section of the complex, bounded by an imposing fortified wall. The gate is flanked by pillars which support a slightly 'pointed' arch above which is a coat of arms with a double-headed eagle motif. The Phokas family claimed descent from the Byzantine Emperor Nikephoros Phokas so incorporated the double-headed eagle into their coat of arms but I am surprised they did not also include the Lion of St. Mark. A small alley to the right of the gate leads behind the complex where there is another small church with some badly defaced and faded frescos on the templon.

If you go back down the way you came, you are a few meters from the main Gythio road or you can take the road which goes south from Karyoupoli and joins the road which leads to Vathy Bay and Ageranos. However, if you continue towards Gythio on the main road, you will come to the important strategic site of Passava.

## PASSAVA CASTLE

Passava Castle dominates the southern cliff where the road to Gythio passes through a narrow gorge. It is not easy to see from the ground, but a substantial part of the castle, especially the curtain walls, still survive.

Passava has been identified as ancient Las which, according to the Iliad, sent a contingent to Troy under the command of Menelaos and which was later a Free Lakonian City according to Pausanias. The hill on which the castle stands was known as Asia and this part of the city was already in ruins when Pausanias visited here, - "The present city is built over the land between three mountains, Ilion, Asia and Knakadion, though it used to stand on the crest of Asia and there are still ruins of the ancient city to this day, with a statue of Herakles in front of the walls and a battle trophy for a victory against Macedonia: the battle was with a detachment of Philip's army when he invaded Lakonia, which had left the main army to devastate the coast. In the ruins is a Temple of Asian Athene."

Philip V of Macedonia looted Lakonia in 218 BC and the description "Asian Athene" is because of the name of the hill. He goes on to say, "At a place called Arainon is the grave of Las, with a statue standing on the tumulus. The people here say this Las was their founder and that he was killed by Achilles." Arainon may be the modern village of Ageranos on Cape Vathy.

Pausanias went on to describe several temples and sanctuaries in the new city and the archaeologist E.S. Forster published a report for the British School at Athens in which he identified the plain south of Passava as the site of the city. This is now agricultural land but several statues were found here as well as Hellenic and Doric masonry.

The castle was built after 1220 by the French Marshal of Achaia to keep the Maniats in check in this area. After the Franks were defeated at Pelagonia in 1259, the castle was occupied by Maniats until 1481 when it was taken by the Turks.

They rebuilt the castle and garrisoned it and it formed part of the defensive chain they established along with Kelefa and Zarnata castles to try and control the Mani. When the Venetians defeated the Turks in 1684, they were allies of the Maniats and had no need of this castle so they destroyed it but when the Turks in turn defeated the Venetians, they rebuilt the castle and held it from 1715 until 1780. They evacuated the castle during the Orlov uprising in 1770 but soon reoccupied it after this disastrous campaign. In 1780, the entire garrison and their families were slaughtered by the Maniats after the arrest and execution of Exarchos Grigorakis who was the head of the powerful clan which was then based at Ageranos and Skoutari. Zanetos Grigorakis took over the leadership of the clan and expanded his power in the area and built a complex at Mavrovouni and a tower on the island of Kranai at Gythio. He was made Bey of the Mani in 1782 so the man behind the massacre of the Turkish Garrison became the Governor on behalf of Turkey a mere two years later!

The Walls of Passava Castle

To reach the castle, you should park at the western edge of the gorge that it defends. There is a signpost for Skamnaki 5 Kms and opposite this, by a house, is an area where you can park off the main road. From here you will see the start of a track which leads round the hill as it climbs. Follow this but it soon runs out and you then have to find your own route to the summit. It is a harder climb than it looks from the ground and wear stout boots and trousers because the 'going' is rough and thorny in places. When you reach the summit, you will see the remains of massive walls and will have to find a gap to enter the grounds of the castle. I found a convenient entrance on the south side. The walls which remain are impressive. They stand about 12 meters high with a parapet running behind the battlements along which you can walk in various places. The grounds of the castle are heavily overgrown and there are mounds of rubble where buildings used to stand. The remains of a large building are in the centre of the area and this, I'm told, used to be a mosque. On the wall which overlooks the gorge there are two towers and from the circular tower on the west side, you have a fantastic panoramic view which clearly shows why this site was chosen as a castle. My fear of heights was severely challenged and, in order to photograph the view down the gorge, I had to 'crawl and cling' my way to this tower! I also encountered two snakes in the grounds and judging by their diamond shaped markings and wide, flat heads, I think they were a poisonous variety. I met an old shepherd on my way back down who, as well as being highly amused by my sweaty and disheveled appearance, agreed that there were a large number of snakes at the castle and by making 'fangs' with his fingers, striking his leg, and then "going all wobbly", he mimed that they were poisonous - so, if you venture up here, be careful and watch where you tread.

## MAVROVOUNI (Melissi)

Traveling on towards Gythio, the countryside changes to fertile valleys and low hills and several roads lead off to the sea on your right with advertisements for Camping Grounds and Hotels. I found nothing of interest along any of these roads until I reached Mavrovouni, 2 kilometers outside Gythio, which is a very obvious hill on your right as you approach Gythio.

Mavrovouni literally means Black Mountain and it was here that Zanetbey Grigorakis built a fortified stronghold called the Goulades or Beanika. It was constructed on the summit in the shape of a trapezium with a strong curtain wall approx 4 meters high. On the SE and SW corners were two round towers between which was an arched gateway and guardhouse. The other two corners were protected by buildings - the NE corner was reinforced with a two storey "palace" which had a parapet around the flat roof and turrets on the corners and the NW corner had a two storey fortified building. This had a double-vaulted ground floor for animals and "official rooms" above it. The palace has completely disappeared and only one of the two vaulted rooms that supported the other building remains. The south wall with the corner towers still stands but the gateway is ruined and the guardhouse destroyed. The complex suffered damage during a Turkish attack in 1803. The Turks had deposed Zanetbey but he was still causing them many problems, so they launched a heavy attack on Gythio and Mavrovouni. The attack failed to defeat Zanetbey although the Turks did destroy some towers. The stronghold was abandoned after 1821. The other tower dwellings at Mavrovouni belonged to the extended Grigorakis family and several remain inhabited to this day.

## GYTHIO

Gythio was an important port in Classical times and the main city of the Free Lakonian League. Pausanias recorded "They have statues of Apollo and Herakles in the market place with Dionysos near them. Elsewhere they have Karneian Apollo and a Sanctuary of Ammon and a bronze statue of Asklepios, with no roof on his temple, and a water spring that belongs to the god and a Sanctuary sacred to Demeter and a statue of Poseidon Earth-Keeper. There are gates here called Kastor's Gates and there is a shrine and statue of Athene in the Akropolis". (Ammon was originally the Libyan god Ammun who became the Egyptian God Amon Ra and was absorbed into Greek culture as Zeus Ammon who had an oracle in the Libyan desert). He went on to say, "The island of Kranai lies offshore of Gythio; Homer says that when Paris carried away Helen, it was on this island he first slept with her."

This is the island of Marathonisi which is now connected to the mainland by a causeway which you pass as you enter Gythio. On the island is the tower of Zanetbey Grigorakis which has been restored and turned into a Mani Museum and there is also a small church which has been built on the foundations of an earlier temple. The museum does not contain "artifacts" from Mani or a great deal about its history but has a display about the various travelers who wrote about Mani over the centuries and some architectural details on various towers and buildings.

Gythio itself consists of mainly neo-classical buildings and more modern houses because it only developed into a town after 1840 and the southern end at Marathonisi was built in 1898. Prior to this, it was little more than a village and most of the classical site, which was situated to the north of Gythio, had disappeared under the sea. You can, however, still see the ruins of a theater at the north end next, to a military barracks, and to find it just follow the signposts in the town.

Gythio has many tavernas and Ouzerias along the edge of the large harbour and it is a pleasant place to stop for refreshments or, if you want to stay here, there are quite a number of apartments or hotel rooms available. There is a wonderful antique shop along the waterfront which you can recognize by a set of huge bellows and a very large copper cauldron which hang outside it, as well as many other bits and pieces on the pavement. It contains many interesting items and although the price-tags are rather frightening, you can persuade the owner to bargain with you!

## AGERANOS

To reach Ageranos, return towards Areopolis for approximately 10 kilometers and, just past Passava, turn left where signs indicate the Belle Helene Hotel and Ageranos Camping. This takes you to Vathy Bay which is a hotchpotch of modern buildings and Hotels which crowd a narrow strip of beach. I suggest you keep going towards the headland at the southern side of the bay.

Pausanias recorded a temple of Artemis Diktynna by the sea on a cape, to the left of which a river flowed into the sea, and this is thought to be this headland. The village of Ageranos is above Cape Vathy, about 4 kilometers from the main road, and in front of the church there used to be a large column which may have come from this temple. Ageranos is also the possible site of the tomb of Las (see Passava Castle).

The village was the stronghold of Antonbey Grigorakis, who was Bey of the Mani from 1803 to 1808, and his nephews also had small strongholds here. The main fortification is east of the main road, just behind the large family church. The tower has an unusual feature in that it is reinforced by a two storey semi-cylinder and the large building on the other side of the courtyard, facing the sea, has a similar projection. The curtain walls are reinforced by the buildings of the complex and by two circular turrets on the N.W. corner of the wall. The tower has been modernised by the addition of a new concrete balcony supported by long concrete legs, which is a great pity because it destroys the clean lines of the tower and, in my opinion, is very ugly.

On the opposite side of the road, the smaller walled complexes of the Bey's nephews parade up the hill in mutually supportive positions which would make any attack on this headland a very formidable task. The topmost complex has an impressive tower which dominates the skyline.

In Leake's time, this village was called Vathy and it was here that the "feud" between two priests took place that Leake recorded and that I have retold in the section on Mani Tradition and Culture.

The road continues round the Cape and drops into another bay. The area is very flat and fertile with a few houses and pensions scattered about. The road follows along the rather desolate beach to a large area of marshy ground at the south of the bay and then climbs up the next headland, Cape Paganea or Cape Kremidara, which forms the northern boundary of Skoutari Bay. The marshy area dries up during the summer but in Spring and Winter it attracts a wide variety of birds.

## KALYVIA

Near the top of the cape, the road forms a Y junction. If you go left this takes you out along the top of the cape through the village of Kalyvia. I cannot find anything of interest about this village but there is a very attractive small harbour on the north shore of Skoutari Bay, just beyond the village.

## SKOUTARI

If you turn right at the Y junction, this road takes you to Skoutari, about 3 kilometers to the west. As you approach Skoutari you will see the village spread out on the side of a hill and running down to a beach.

On your right, before reaching the village is what I think must have been a fairly large monastery but I can find no information about it. There is a domed, cruciform church with a bell tower and inside there are some blackened and faded frescos. One of these has an unusual feature in that the halo which encircles the Virgin's head is made of rosettes done in relief in either plaster or carved marble. (I couldn't tell because of discolouration). Next to the church are the ruins of a large, three storey building with arched windows and an arched door protected by a Petramachos. At right angles to this and forming a small square with the church on the other side, is a smaller, two storey building. On the western side of this 'square' is a large Liakos which I think may have been a gateway but it is very difficult to tell for certain. There are also the ruins of other buildings within the complex but only the foundations remain.

The Monastery of Skoutari

At a distance of about 100 meters to the East is another small church with a barrel vaulted roof and a few faded frescos on the templon.

As you enter Skoutari there is a ruined church on your left with very little inside except rubble. There is a small circuit route round Skoutari which takes you past many ruined houses and towers. There is a large, newish church near to a ruined tower, of which only a corner fragment remains, but down below this church is another smaller church with damaged frescos inside.

Just past here is a square with a war memorial and a ruined tower which a local told me was that of Katsanos. If that is accurate, it is the tower which Leake described as harbouring many fleas etc when he stayed there. (see Mesa Mani -

Land of Evil Counsel). Near to this is a small, double church but it was locked. If you head down towards the beach, you pass an unusual tower in that it is sandwiched between two houses.

The beach is a wonderful, sandy stretch with a pleasant taverna at one end and a small harbour at the other and looks out over the extensive and well sheltered Bay of Skoutari. Right on the edge of the beach is a small, domed church dedicated to St. Barbara with a few remaining frescos inside. The archaeologist E.S. Forster argues that Skoutari is the probable site of ancient Asine which was besieged by Philip V of Macedonia although he failed to capture it. He states, "There are distinct traces of Roman buildings near the sea and a number of ancient blocks and columns built into the modern village". Pausanias didn't come this way so we cannot rely on him for an identification and not all archaeologists agree with Forster.

There is now a road which takes you round the southern shore of the bay and eventually reaches Kotronas (see Mani Circuit). However, it is not yet finished and very rough in places so beware of the risk of damage to your car if you decide to go this way.

## PARASIROS

If you travel back through Skoutari and turn left where the signpost indicates Gythio, you travel a short distance until you come to a turnoff on the left to the village of Parasiros, 3 kilometers from Skoutari. You can see the village on the hillside and a winding road takes you up to it. There are some older, fortified houses in the village but it consists mainly of more recent, concrete built houses and I found nothing of particular interest. On the edge of the village, you pass a small church with a concrete shelter over the door and this has a few faded frescos on the templon and part of a wall.

The only way out from Parasiros is back to where you turned off, turn left and then follow the road which takes you back to the main Gythio road which you rejoin just east of Karyoupoli.

# BARDOUNIA

The area of Bardounia is north of the Areopolis to Gythio road on the eastern side of the Taygetos Mountains and as far north as Arna. The name comes from a castle which was built by the Byzantine Princes from Mystras near the village of Agios Nikolaos. This had already been abandoned by the early 1800's and Leake recorded that the last occupants had been the Venetians about one hundred years earlier.

This is such a large area, with a myriad of roads, that I have only covered some of the routes in the area - you can explore any others that take your fancy. Many of the villages are very similar, being newer houses built where there were originally only isolated, fortified houses, so I do not go into detail except where I have discovered some history or an interesting feature. The journey time from Stoupa and Exo Mani means that this area is better explored from a base at Gythio or nearby, if you want to cover it fully.

The Turkish occupation of Mystras and the Lakonian plain meant that much of the area was sparsely occupied by the Greeks - the Taygetos offering more security. Following the Turkish defeat of the Venetians in 1715, the area was systematically colonized by the war-like, Moslem Albanians and there was another influx of Albanians in 1770, following the disastrous Orlov inspired revolt. These were brought in to help quell the uprising but by 1779 they had become a serious threat to the Turks themselves who enlisted the support of the Klephts and other Greeks to push them out of the Peloponnese.

In one of the strange anomalies that happened in this period, Kolokotronis's father, Kostantes, was enlisted by the Kapitan Pasha , Hassan Gazi, (Hassan The Conqueror) to expel the Albanians from Messinia. They fought a large battle near Tripoli and, according to Kolokotronis, only seven hundred Albanians escaped from a force of twelve thousand! "They built up a tower at Tripolitsa with the heads of these Albanians and the Peloponnese was at peace for a time." The following year Hassan Gazi sent a force against Kostantes Kolokotronis, his erstwhile ally,  and he was killed at Mikri Kastania in Bardounia. (see below)

The settlement of Albanians in Bardounia was mainly in the more fertile areas in the south and east while the Maniats held onto the western villages on the slopes of Taygetos. Col. Leake never visited this area but he listed the various villages which were mainly occupied by Turks and Albanians under the overall control of Amus Aga. "The Musulmans fight among each other like the Maniats but at present Amus Aga keeps affairs tolerably quiet."

In 1780, when the Maniats retaliated for the death of Exarchos Grigorakis and massacred the garrison at Passava, they also killed or drove out most of the Turkish Albanians in the south of Bardounia and re-occupied the western part of the area as far north as Arna.

## SKAMNAKI

As you approach the gorge at Passava on the main road to Gythio, there is a sign showing Skamnaki - 5 Kms off to the left. The road starts reasonably but becomes rough track in some places. The village is one that is still typically Maniat with a few towers and defensive houses and a number of newer buildings. Leake reported, "At Skamnaki, ancient coins and sepulchres are said to be found." There is a possibility that the area around here was the site of ancient Hypsi where Pausanias described "a sanctuary of Asklepios and Artemis of the Bay Tree" but there has not been a positive identification.

## PASSAVA TO EGIES VIA SIDEROKASTRO

Two hundred meters past the road to Skamnaki, just opposite the gorge below Passava Castle, is a road to your left signposted Karvelas, Mirsini, Siderokastro and a few other place names.

The first village you come to is Karvelas, about 5 kilometers from the main road, on a hill on your left, and just past here you can see Skamnaki on the hillside in the distance to the west. A little further on, the road forks with Mirsini to the left and Konakia to the right. Turn left here and after driving 2 kilometers, you come to Mirsini. This has several old fortified houses and a large church dedicated to St. Spiridon. Drive past this church along a narrow, slightly rough road to the outskirts of the village and you will see an isolated tower and a few houses on a hill to your left. This is typical of how most of the area of Bardounia looked prior to the more recent expansion of the villages.

Continue along this road towards the mountains and you can see another isolated village, Tombra, on a hilltop with some very large defensive houses. Just a little further on you pass through a small village, Skyfianika, and then there is a road junction with a track leading up to Tombra. This is a rough track higher up the hill so you really need a 4x4 to reach the village.

If you carry straight on from this junction, the road deteriorates but is still driveable and you climb high up the mountains to the village of Siderokastro. This village is spread along the road which has a turnoff signposted to Poliaravos and Misochori and another junction further on to Skifianika and Skamnitsa.

I wanted to go to Poliaravos because this was the site of Ibrahim Pasha's final attempt to invade the Mani in August 1826 - after his failures in Verga and Pyrgos Dirou in June of that year - so I set off towards the village but the track deteriorated so badly that I was forced to stop. I was in my beaten-up old Peugeot which, although it has taken me to many extreme places, could not handle this track! Through binoculars I could see a small hamlet high above me with stone houses and towers which blended so well with the rocky slopes that they were difficult to make out and I think this was Poliaravos. The Egyptian army would have been seen approaching from a long way off and it was no wonder to me that the Maniats selected this site to oppose it. The invading force was defeated and withdrew back to the plains of Lakonia and abandoned any further ideas of subduing the Maniats.

You should return the way you came and take the other road to Konakia. This suddenly narrows next to a church on your right. This was locked but has a fresco of St. George over a doorway. The narrow concrete road brings you to a T-junction and if you turn left, you will see the small village of Pilala on a small hill with the dome of a church and a tower. The Xatzakos tower is a substantial building and has a plaque dating it 1776. Despite the addition of a concrete balcony, concrete battlements and a metal chimney protruding from a wall at a jaunty angle, it is still an impressive building.

Xatzakos Tower - Pilala

Below one wall is an old cannon which has been mounted on wheels made from the old grindstones of an olive press. If you carry on through the village, the track becomes very rough and eventually takes you back to the road which leads to Siderokastro.

The village to the right of the T-junction is Konakia which has a large, restored church and some defensive houses. The road continues past the village and winds for some distance through wooded hills to the village of Platanos. From here, you can drive to Melissa via Krini but, unless you are in a 4x4 - don't! You should take the road to the right which eventually brings you to the main road from Gythio to Sparta and turn left to reach Egies.

## MARATHEA TO EGIES

If you don't want to go the above route but want to avoid Gythio, then follow the main Areopolis road east for 15 kilometers until you see a sign for Marathea on your left. Don't follow the track to the village but stay on the surfaced road which takes you over a "Bailey" bridge, through Agios Vasilios and onto the Sparta road. Drive north from here to reach Egies.

## EGIES to MIKRI KASTANIA and GIATRISSA

Traveling north from Gythio on the main road to Sparta for about 8 kilometers, you come to Egies which is sprawled along the main road. There is a road off to your left with a signpost showing many villages including Melissa, Agios Nikolaos, Kastania and Giatrissa.

The road follows a wide, fertile valley with scattered farms and citrus and olive trees on either side of a rocky stream. The valley gradually narrows and you cross a bridge with the village of Archonliko off to your left. You then climb higher into the hills with glimpses of villages on the hillsides and the Taygetos rising in the distance. The road passes through the villages of Melissa and Kokkina Louria which both have a few older houses and many new ones. Both villages also have large churches which have been modernised.

The road continues to climb and you will see in the distance, off to your right, the ruins of Bardounia Castle on a rocky hilltop - at least I think it is Bardounia Castle. It is just outside the village of Agios Nikolaos, about 15 kilometers from the Gythio road, and when I tried to confirm the name, I was told it was just called "To Kastro - The Castle". It is a steep climb up to the ruins and there is not a great deal to see as it has been abandoned for some considerable time but it looks very picturesque on its craggy hilltop.

The road continues to climb higher after you leave Agios Nikolaos and you can see the monastery of Panagia Giatrissa on the skyline on the top of the mountains. You pass a turnoff to Selegoudi on your right but I found nothing of particular interest here either.

## MIKRI KASTANIA

Mikri Kastania is 5 kilometers further on and looks like a typical Maniat village and you can see fortified houses and a couple of towers as you pass an astonishing memorial on the outskirts of the village. A carved marble facade shows the "sortie" described below with the Maniat families, including women, children and a priest, charging the Turkish troops who are depicted wearing their "turned up" shoes or slippers. You will also see a couple of the cannonballs of which Kolokotronis is so disparaging.

The village is known as Mikri Kastania to distinguish it from the Kastania which is on the western slopes of the mountains above Stoupa (see Exo Mani). This is the place where Kolokotronis's father Kostantes was fatally wounded defending one of the towers of Panayotaros Venetsanakis. He and Panayotaros were defending one tower while Panayotaros's eighty year old father held another. They were called upon to surrender and give up one of their sons each to be held as hostages, whereupon they would be allowed to go free, but they refused. Theodoros Kolokotronis, a young teenager at the time, was with his father and later recorded, "The Turkish army then prepared to besiege them vigourously; they brought up cannon and bombs and poured upon them an unceasing fire both by night and day. Their bombs and their cannons however, did not inspire the besieged with any dread and for twelve nights and for twelve days they stood out nobly and bravely."

They were hoping for help from elsewhere in the Mani but when none came, they decided to sortie from the tower and escape. Kostantes Kolokotronis and two of his brothers, Apostoles and Giorgos were killed; his other brother, Anagnostes escaped with Theodoros Kolokotronis; some children including two of Theodoros's little brothers were captured as was Panayotaros but, while the children were spared, Panayotaros was executed. His father stayed defending his tower but was eventually captured alive and hanged after his hands and feet were cut off.

The two towers can still be seen in the village. One stands high above the village on the south side and the other is on the north side, just beyond and above the small square. The latter was in fact two fortified houses, one of two stories and the other three stories, enclosed in a defensive wall and connected by a stone bridge which ran between them on the second floor, so it was more like a small castle than a tower. This "castle" is being restored and will be used as a museum and accommodation for visitors but may not be ready for use until late 1998.

From the small square, the road continues towards the monastery of Panagia Giatrissa. This road has just been surfaced all the way to the top and it is worth going up there just for the views. The Monastery sits on the watershed of the Taygetos and you can see both east and west of the mountain range and the village far below you to the west is Milia (see Exo Mani). The monastery itself is a sprawling, concrete maze of rooms and the main church is modern inside with some earlier, carved door surrounds. There is also a large Gynaikonitis or women's' gallery.

From here, you must return to the main road the same way you came. Do not be tempted to follow the track which leads north from here along the ridge unless you are in a 4x4. In an ordinary car you will get into serious difficulties but in a 4x4 it is possible to drive all the way to the Forest of Vasiliki and then down the mountains to Saidona in Exo Mani. It is a fantastic journey with stunning scenery and worth hiring a 4x4 for the experience.

## EGIES TO ARNA

The signs for Petrina, Meletini and Arna are further along the main road to Sparta, past the turnoff for Mikri Kastania, in the village of Egies. The road climbs into the hills through the villages of Petrina, Lemonia and Melitini to Agia Marina.

## AGIA MARINA

The signpost for the village shows that it was also known as Tseria and Leake referred to this village as having two towers and thirty houses - all inhabited by Turks. I could not find any remains of the towers and there are quite a number of new houses here.

As you leave the village you can see an old church on the top of a wooded hill across a small valley on your left. A track which leads from the edge of the village goes down into this valley and up to the church but is not very suitable for cars. I was delighted when I spotted this church as it was the only one I had seen which might compare with the Byzantine churches of Exo and Mesa Mani but when I reached it I was more than a little disappointed.

I'm sure it is a Byzantine church but it is in very bad condition inside and out. The roof tiles are all gone and much of the stonework is crumbling, especially around the window which faces south where the tiles of the cloisonné brickwork are exposed like jagged teeth. Inside, the space is taken up by wooden scaffolding which may be needed to keep the building from falling down or may be signs that restoration is planned. The frescos that remain are obscure and hard to decipher but they could be saved and would transform the church back to some of its former glory. Outside there was further evidence of neglect where a few broken boxes containing the disinterred bones of someone's ancestors had been dumped against a wall. It is in a beautiful setting, enclosed in a stone wall on a small spur above the valley with Cypress trees growing in the churchyard but its neglected state made my heart ache

## ARNA

My spirits were lifted again when I reached Arna. It is a beautiful village which spreads out on the mountain side and I parked in the small, tree-shaded square with a spectacular view over the valleys below and glimpses of far away villages. I went into the Kafeneon and had no sooner sat down than I was engaged in conversion by the elderly people on the next table. Within minutes I was urged to join them and we shared wine, food and conversation in my broken Greek and their broken English. We discussed Kolokotronis, the Turks (then and now), the EEC, the Royal Family, compared the weather in Greece to that in the UK and I was shown the photographs of grandchildren far away in the USA and in Australia. More people joined in the conversation, we had some more wine and a great time putting the world to rights but I had to leave while I could still drive my car! My attempts to pay were futile and I left the village with a sore hand from all the farewell handshakes. It was a wonderful example of the warmth and hospitality for which the Greeks are renowned and which I experience so often in the Mani.

There is a road which is signposted from this square to Agios Nikolaos and Mikri Kastania but it is definitely only driveable in a 4x4 - so go back to the Lakonian plain by the same route.

# BIBLIOGRAPHY

This list is not in any particular order and includes some books I have not yet found but which I am given to believe are worth reading. Some books are out of print but you may find them in a library. There are several books about Mani published in Greek but I cannot read them and have not included them.

1."Mani, Travels in the Southern Peloponnese" - P. L. Fermor
Probably the best known book about the area.

2. "Deep Into Mani" - P. Greenhalgh & E. Eliopoulos
An excellent account of exploration in Mesa Mani - especially churches.
Out of print.

3."Mani" - Yanis Saitas. (A volume from a series - Greek Traditional Architecture).
Published in Athens by "Melissa". A detailed study of towers and buildings and relevant history. Well illustrated.

4. "Mani, History and Monuments" - D. Eliopoulou-Rogan
A useful reference for Churches, Historical Sites and History.
Out of Print.

5. "Travels in the Morea" - W.M. Leake
A wonderful account of Mani in 1805 - just prior to the War of Independence.
Out of Print.

6. "Reminiscences of Athens and the Morea." - Earl of Carnarvon
Post War of Independence (1839) account of travels in Mani.
Out of Print

7. "Kolokotrones. The Klepht and the Warrior. Sixty Years of Peril and Daring. An Autobiography." - Translated by E. M. Edmonds
His memoirs as dictated to G. Tertzetis. Somewhat hard to follow but fascinating.
Out of Print.

8. "Guide to Greece" - Pausanias.
Many versions exist but I recommend Penguin Classics Vols: 1& 2 translated by P. Levi. Only a small part is relevant to Mani in Vol 2 but both volumes are worth reading.

9. "Castles of the Morea" - K. Andrews.
I haven't read it but it is highly commended.

10. "Account of a Journey through the district of Maina, in The Morea" - J.B.S. Morritt.
I cannot find this (yet) but worth reading.

11. "Annual of the British School at Athens." Various reports by archaeologists from the School.
I am grateful to the School for allowing me to use their library and it was here that I read original copies of Leake & Carnarvon which are kept under 'lock & key'.

12. "Pictures of the Mani" - A. A. Parkins
An account of a 'walk' through Mani by an American artist. Her pen & ink drawings capture the Mani in wonderful detail and atmosphere. Published in Athens in 1971. Out of Print?
(My thanks to 'Theo' who gave me a copy as a Christmas present in 1996).

13. "The Mani Peninsula - Treasures and Austerity" - A. & J. Ioannou.
I found this book rather confusing (especially trying to relate text to photos and to a rather inaccurate map) but it did help me to find some beautiful churches.
Printed privately (I think) in Paris, it is still available locally in Mani.

# INDEX OF TOWNS & VILLAGES

| | | | |
|---|---|---|---|
| Lagia | 71 | Prosilio | 31 |
| Lakos | 38 | Pyrgos | 42 |
| Limeni | 57 | Pyrgos Dirou | 63 |
| Liontaki | 68 | Pyrrichos | 74 |
| Loukadika | 74 | Riglia | 49 |
| Malta | 29 | Saidona | 44 |
| Marathea | 104 | Siderokastro | 102 |
| Marmari | 89 | Skamnaki | 102 |
| Mavrovouni | 96 | Skoutari | 99 |
| Megali Mantinia | 23 | Skyfianika | 102 |
| Melissa | 104 | Sotirianika | 22 |
| Mezapos | 64 | Stavri | 81 |
| Mikri Kastania | 105 | Stavropigio | 27 |
| Milia | 46 | Stoupa | 39 |
| Mina | 77 | Thalames | 52 |
| Mountanistika | 68 | Tigani | 64 |
| Neochori | 41 | Tourloti | 80 |
| Neochori (Mesa) | 92 | Trachila | 48 |
| Nomia | 66 | Trikotsova | 22 |
| Nomitsi | 50 | Trissakia | 77 |
| Nyfi | 73 | Tseria | 31 |
| Ochia | 83 | Tsigou | 56 |
| Oitylo | 55 | Tsikalia | 70 |
| Paliros | 89 | Tsopakos | 77 |
| Parasiros | 100 | Vachos | 92 |
| Passava | 94 | Vamvaka | 77 |
| Pedino | 31 | Vathia | 87 |
| Pigi | 49 | Verga | 21 |
| Pilala | 103 | Vorio | 26 |
| Platsa | 50 | Zarnata | 27 |
| Poliaravos | 102 | | |
| Porto Kayio | 87 | | |
| Proastio | 37 | | |

# ANTONIS THOMEAS SERVICES

**Stoupa-Lektron**

**240 24 Agios Nikolaos**

**Messinia**

**Greece**

Tel: +30 721 77689 - Fax: +30 721 77571

E-Mail :- antthom@otenet.gr

*We provide the following services:-*

Foreign Exchange

Car Hire

Competitive rates for long term and pre-booked car hire.

Fax/E-mail us for more information & prices

Tourist Information

Telephone & Fax Services

Office Facilities for Tour Companies

*Arrangements for Independent Travelers seeking*

*long-term or Out-of-Season Accommodation*

*Fax/E-mail us for more information*

# Real Estate Office

Houses for sale in the district
Land for sale with building permission
Architects and Builders arranged
Construction supervised to your specifications

The office is situated at the southern end of Stoupa Bay - just past Akrogiali Taverna which overlooks the harbour.

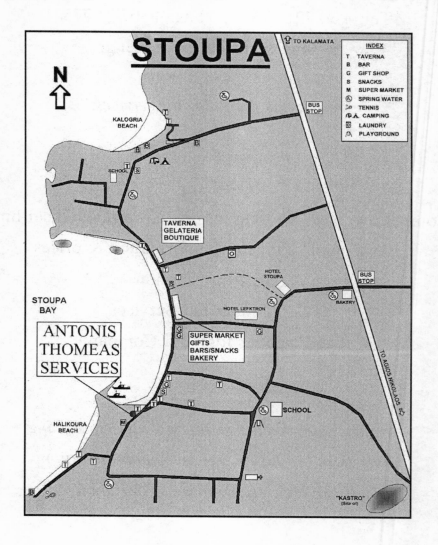